Football Fans

in their own write...

Football Fans
in their own write...

David Picken

All author proceeds from the sale of this book will be donated to UNICEF.

First published in 2023 by Fair Play Publishing
PO Box 4101, Balgowlah Heights, NSW 2093, Australia

www.fairplaypublishing.com.au
ISBN: 978-1-925914-75-7
ISBN:978-1-925914-76-4 (ePub)

Cover design and typesetting by Leslie Priestley

All inquiries should be made to the Publisher via hello@fairplaypublishing.com.au

A catalogue record of this book is available from the National Library of Australia.

Contents

Introduction

Why? How? If?

This book is a showcase of football fans describing their passion for football: what fires that passion and what keeps the flame burning? Football—or soccer, as some would have it—the round ball game, Association Football, the World Game, the Global Game. Not completely, but very largely, it is a game played with the feet, so I call it 'football' and that is the term I will use from now on. The shorthand title I have adopted for the book in the text is *Football Fans*.

I have had the idea of this book in my head for a long time. Followers of a particular club will often know at least the famous people who follow their club. They are just rank-and-file football fans like the rest of us.

Football fandom is a great leveller. Most often, though of course not always, you are born to the club you follow and support. Traditionally, you don't get to choose. This is changing in the modern era—many people now choose on perceived entertainment value or choose on an already established level of success. However, there is still a strong thread of the club choosing you. You follow the team that your mum or dad follow or the team that has long been established where you were born and grew up. Put simply, it's tribal.

And so my basic, initial idea was: How about a book that collects stories by these famous people describing their passion for the clubs that they follow? I wanted to invite them to write about the special memories that give expression to their passion.

Having established that basic picture I am assuming that many readers' immediate thoughts will turn to the question of: *How do you make such a thing happen? How do you recruit the contributors?* There is a story to this all by itself.

First, let me describe how the book is set out. Each chapter or section is dedicated to a particular contributor. Their piece, in homage to the club they support, is preceded by my introduction to the contributor. I have aimed at making each 'intro' like a mini bio. The only exception to this basic 'shape' is the chapter on Sunderland AFC by the triple Oscar-winning lyricist (writer of those great songs from *Jesus Christ Superstar*, *Evita*, *The Lion King*, etc.), Sir Tim Rice. Sir Tim preferred to write the introduction himself. Footnotes in each piece are by me.

So—OK, I am writing the introductions but really the 'meat' of the book belongs to the contributors. I don't think of it as my book. I am just the 'ringmaster' assembling and presenting 'the talent'. Right here you should know that all the royalties will be donated to UNICEF, the United Nations Children's Charity.

Some of the people who feature in this book are well known, some even *very* well known. Some are very famous. Some are a bit famous. Some are not famous. They all share one characteristic: they are football fans and enthusiastically, passionately so. Famous or not, the gut feeling of the thrill of supporting your football team is the same. The unbridled joy of a win; the deep anguish of a loss—same!

Who are the contributors? As it became clear to me as to what might be possible the idea evolved. Yes, I wanted to recruit some 'celebrity' fans and I have. However, I grew to realise that the book could still work by assembling a list of contributors who are passionate about football by any measure and have their own notability and worthiness. I realised that the book could show the broad cross-section that characterises football fans across the world.

So, if not fame in the orthodox sense, what are the qualifying criteria? Numbers? Triple Oscar winner? I think we can say that Sir Tim Rice is famous. Three Oscars—in the vernacular, good stats.

Let me tell you, though, that the unsung heroes, those not-so-famous folks, among the other contributors have their own very impressive numbers.

Try these. Just random selections here ... Australian Brendan Schwab heads up the World Players' Association (responsible for 85,000 athletes in all manner of sports in 60 countries)—why is he such an enthusiastic follower of English club Aston Villa? Vicki Morton—gives her life and soul to South Hobart Football Club in Tasmania, and in her broader football volunteering in the administration of the game she covers 40,000 footballers across Australia. She is a founding member of Women in Football Australia. My friend Jean Jackson writes about three clubs, including Port Vale. She and her husband volunteer at the Vale. She has written upwards of 600 pieces for the match day program, and they travel over 16,000 kilometres a season to attend matches. Impressive stats. Passionate. They all have fascinating stories.

And that leads me to note that just as the book is not full of celebrity fans, it is also not necessarily about glamorous teams.

For me, the 'magic combo' would be 'famous person follows not nearly so famous club'. They don't change their colours and go for a famous team to match, arguably, their public persona. Following a football team is a deeper thing than that. If you follow a team and it really means something to you, it's nothing to do with fame (yours or the club's). It's in your bones—forever. We have more than a couple of those folk with the magic combo.

What I have aimed to show is the broad, rich spectrum of people that follow football and follow it with a passion. I hope you will agree it is a rich tapestry. I hope when you see the list of contributors and the piece that they have written you will be surprised - and, I hope, pleasantly so.

Famous fans are just like us, and their passion can prompt unusual behaviour. You may know the story about singer/songwriter Elvis Costello being very late onstage for a concert at a university in Norwich in England on the evening of May 25, 2005. I'm not sure if he makes a habit of being late, but on this night, we could argue he had a good excuse. He could not tear himself away from the TV in the university common room. He was watching the game that became known as the Miracle of Istanbul. His beloved Liverpool FC, playing AC Milan in the

Champions League Final, were 3–0 down at half time. They came back and levelled it. Extra time was to come but Elvis could delay the concert no longer and took the stage. Liverpool won in a dramatic penalty shoot-out!

Let's have some recruitment stories. Wins and losses.

Those who have agreed to contribute have done so enthusiastically and often touchingly.

An element of the process which gave me great pleasure was when I received a contribution which moved me to ask the contributor if they had ever written down their recollections before. I was enchanted by what they had written and, intuitively, I felt as if I knew the answer—and every time I asked that question the answer was something like, "*Do you know, I haven't. I have held this story in my heart, but no-one has ever asked me to write it down until you did.*"

Henry Winter, highly regarded journalist and Chief Football Writer for *The Times* newspaper in London, surprised me and, so to speak, 'gazumped' me all at the same time. I wrote to Henry asking him if he would be prepared to write the Foreword to the book. It was very much in the manner of in-for-a-penny-in-for-a-pound/don't-ask-never-know kind of thing. "Oh no," he replied. "I want to be in the main thing—I'll do a piece on following England." The words 'chuffed' and 'bits' sprang to mind!

I want to impress you with some of the declines—I'm proud to have had replies from some very famous people. Let me tell you that in my 'box of treasures' (the recruitment section of my research file) I have letters from Emmanuel Macron (Olympique de Marseille), Angela Merkel (FC Cottbus) and Prince William (Aston Villa)—yes, on Buckingham Palace letterhead. All replied at length. Little victories, I call them.

More than little was the victory in the reply from the Archbishop of Canterbury, Justin Welby (Sunderland). Unable to contribute himself but, in wishing me well, recommended that maybe the Church of England's lead Bishop for Sport, Libby Lane (Manchester United) might be better placed.

We do have a former member of Australia's national women's side, the Matildas, on the team—Heather Garriock (Heart of Midlothian). Thank you,

Heather. I tried several others without success. Melissa Barbieri, legendary Matildas goalie (86 caps), was helpful and would have loved to contribute but couldn't. Here's a little-known fact—as a youngster Melissa didn't follow football at all and she doesn't have a favourite team. Basketball was her game and Michael Jordan is her hero.

We also have a former world champion in squash. Check out Angela Smith's section for a special Australian connection too!

I took heart from replies that both made a special point of regaling the project and explaining what commitments they had that would preclude them from contributing.

Did I need to know that Michael Palin (Sheffield Wednesday) is heavily involved (writing and filming) in a new TV series? *Something for us to look forward to*, I thought. Why tell me that actor Keira Knightley (West Ham) is busy filming in Boston (USA) otherwise she would have loved to contribute. The reply from 'Parky', Sir Michael Parkinson (Barnsley), was at length to praise the project and explain that his current commitments were just too heavy for him to contribute. Australian singer Jimmy Barnes (Rangers) thought it was a fascinating project but, regrettably, just "*didn't have the bandwidth*" in the foreseeable future. Stephen Fry (Norwich) was another who loved the idea but was just too busy with various writing and media projects. Actor Robert Carlyle (Rangers)—remember him from TV's *Hamish Macbeth* and the movies *Trainspotting* and *The Full Monty*? Likewise, actor Tom Hiddleston (Rangers) and the Mayor of London, Sadiq Khan (Liverpool), loved the idea and were kind enough to let me know why they couldn't help.

I do want to mention author Tim Parks. Many aficionados of football books and books in general will know *A Season with Verona,* Tim's compelling story of following Hellas Verona, home and away, for a whole season. I contacted Tim through his website. He replied most graciously and generously. It would have been great to have him involved but he asked to be excused, commenting that, "*I think I've said all I want to say about football.*"

Whilst some names were identified from a broad-brush 'celebrity football fans' Google search, others were the result of out-and-out intuitive guesses. I would see someone on TV and sort of think, completely off the cuff, *Hmmm ... I wonder if they are a football supporter?* then do a more specific search.

Once I had a name connected to a club, one technique I used and that bore fruit was to contact the administration at the club. Colin Garlick, the CEO at my club, Port Vale, was very helpful in providing names and contact details and in his encouragement to try this approach.

One name he gave me was that of his opposite number at Hull City. I had identified that the actor Sir Tom Courtenay was the president of Hull's supporters' club. My contact put me in touch with the supporters' club chair, Kathryn Townsley. Rather than making the proverbial 'executive decision', Kathryn assured me she could get the enquiry sent to Sir Tom. He was only too pleased to contribute, and I think he produced a thoroughly charming piece. If you are a movie buff you will know that one of his movies was the 60s classic *Dr Zhivago*—yes, Sir Tom does mention Omar Sharif in his piece!

Another example is learning that highly regarded film director Ken Loach is a fan of Bath City (a team in the sixth tier in England). The Bath City administrative staff put me in touch with Ken. Immediate response: "*I'd be very pleased to contribute*."

Eric Knowles, one of the experts who appears on the *Antiques Roadshow* TV program, has his own website and it became clear that he answers the 'Contact us' enquiries. "*Hello David, I would be delighted to explain my support for Burnley FC (my tribal team)...*". I love the word 'explain'! A great thrill to receive these replies.

I don't have any American contributors. I wish I did. I found contacts for and tried several and what I can tell you is that they win the prize for warmth and politeness. All replied and I'll give you just two examples—both Liverpool fans. Basketball legend Steve Kerr—both as a player with the multiple championship-winning Chicago Bulls and as a coach with the Golden State Warriors. Nice guy. Ice hockey star Alexander Ovechkin—likewise. Thank you, respectively, agents Julie Magrane and David Arbrutyn.

How did I do it? I like to think I've earned the middle name of 'Resourceful'.

My basic technique was to send an email to a person I had identified as a possible intermediary. This email was concise—basic idea of the project, indicate all royalties to charity and stress that I'm not looking for personal contact details. Ask them to check whether I could send a formal invitation. I devised a formal invitation letter where I demonstrated knowledge of the football club followed. My suggestion was that contributors focus on the club they support. And that they could, for example, write about a memorable season, a memorable game, a favourite player, or simply explain how they became a supporter and why they remain so. Some contributors covered all of that—only a few contributors took a more general perspective in describing what sparked their interest in football in the first place. Whatever, each one had a 'football story'—the tale of: *'How and why does the game captivate me?'*

I've told you that I've had the idea brewing for a while, but what was that special moment that sparked me into action?

In 2013 Cardinal Jorge Bergoglio of Argentina was elected to become Pope Francis. It was shortly after this that I first started to think seriously that I might have a go at making a book out of the idea.

I hear you: What has that got to do with anything?

In that year, I attended Christmas Eve mass with my wife and daughters in a small town in South Australia about 80 kilometres north of the state capital Adelaide. The priest was very clever in his opening remarks to welcome the congregation. He had done his research. *"I'd just like to point out,"* he said, *"that our new pope is a Crows supporter."* There were smiles all round and people inched towards the edge of their seats.

The Adelaide Crows are the first team from South Australia to compete in the Australian Rules football national competition - a different football code. Pope Francis is an enthusiastic follower of a football team from a Buenos Aires suburb—San Lorenzo de Almagro. The nickname of San Lorenzo is *Los Cuervos*, The Crows. It was a while before I did anything substantial about it, but that experience is what breathed life into the idea.

You can send an email to the pope—@vatican.va—no luck! I guess he gets thousands of emails every day and an army of people to field them. Maybe the odd one gets through to his close offsiders; even fewer will be read by the man himself. I suspect mine was ... ahem ... *filed!* Then I was told that Pope Francis prefers to receive old-fashioned letters on paper.

I sought the help of a senior cleric in the Catholic Church hierarchy in Australia: *"Can you help me to send a letter to the Pope?"* Full background and rationale. I told them my Adelaide Crows story. I even told them I had the Church of England on board at a very high level. My thinking being, *So, how about you blokes? Let's mend the Henry VIII schism!* sort of style. I gave them an alternative: Cardinal Tarcisio Bertone—Juventus supporter. No good: "*The Archbishop cannot accommodate this enquiry.*"

As well as knowing that Pope Francis was a Crows supporter there was something else that spurred me. I learned that he really was a passionate, rusted-on supporter. If he couldn't attend games, he loved watching his beloved San Lorenzo live on TV. As an act of supreme self-denial after becoming Pope, he declared that he would no longer watch games live. I thought, *this bloke is serious.* So I thought I'd give the San Lorenzo club president a 'go'. Even included a Spanish translation of my letter. "*Estimado Señor Presidente ...*"

No luck, no reply. Eventually, I did find a way of getting my request a good way along the line. Archbishop Charles Balvo is the Apostolic Nuncio in Canberra—he's like the Vatican's ambassador to Australia. He agreed—in his reply to me, he wrote, "*I'd love to help ... I think it's worth a try at least.*" I like to believe Archbishop Balvo 'got it'. He agreed to forward my letter to the Vatican. *Hope springs eternal*, I thought, though not with any great confidence. *Let's hope we at least get a reply for the 'box of treasures'*. It took a long time but eventually I received a reply from Monsignor Sánchez de Toca, a minister in the Dicastery for Culture and Education. The Holy Father suggests—he's read the letter!!—that we use what he calls his Lay Encyclical on Sport. So that is what we have—it is in the form of an interview conducted by the famous Italian sports newspaper *La Gazetta dello Sport.*

Yes, Pope Francis is one of our contributors.

Talking of translations, I got a Brazilian friend to translate my formal invitation letter into Portuguese. I sent it to the all-time great player Marta, c/o Miami Pride. No reply. I have discovered since from someone who is a close friend of the Miami Pride club president that Marta is a very shy and private person. She is excused!

Yes, in case you are wondering, it is well known that Australian tennis great Ash Barty is a Liverpool fan. I did contact her agent—nice reply.

Football plays an important role in the lives of many people. There was a time when a large proportion of a football crowd were working people. Various phrases were, and indeed are still, bandied around—the working man's (and working woman's) ballet, the people's game ('the people' being the rank and file) are just two. Today the cross-section of a football crowd cuts across many social classes.

Who are the *Football Fans*? Stick figures they may be, but even so there are still all shapes and sizes. Just who are the people in L. S. Lowry's painting *Going To The Match*?

Let's bring this introduction towards a close with the words of the wise.

"All that I know most surely about morality and obligations I owe to football."

Albert Camus

"'Five days shalt thou labour,' as the Bible says. The seventh day is the Lord thy God's. The sixth day is for football."

Anthony Burgess

"OK, publishing a book and releasing a movie is all very well, but Tottenham beating Man United ... priceless."

Salman Rushdie

"Life itself is a game of football."

Sir Walter Scott

"The goalkeeper is the lone eagle, the man of mystery, the last defender."

Vladimir Nabokov

"I fell in love with football just as I was later to fall in love with women: suddenly, inexplicably, uncritically, giving no thought to the pain or disruption it would bring with it."

Nick Hornby

"In a football match everything is complicated by the presence of the other team."

Jean Paul Sartre

"Chelsea scored twice while I was on the Tube, so my departure was a stroke of tactical genius that Jose Mourinho failed to acknowledge."

Roddy Doyle

Arts and Entertainment

Sir Tom Courtenay
(Hull City FC)—Actor

If you make a list of leading British actors of a similar age range as Tom Courtenay, you will see that it is a veritable roll of honour. Each era has its greats, of course, but this was a golden age and Tom Courtenay sits alongside contemporaries such as Michael Caine, Albert Finney and Peter O'Toole, to name but three.

He trained at the Royal Academy for Dramatic Arts and has been active in theatre, film, television and radio from 1960 to the present date.

My first recollection of him was his leading role in *The Loneliness of the Long Distance Runner* (1962) which brought his first BAFTA. He played the title role in *Billy Liar* (1963), first on the stage and then in the film. For me a particular favourite was Lieutenant Robin Grey in *King Rat* (1965). An Oscar nomination for Best Supporting Actor came for his performance alongside Omar Sharif in *Doctor Zhivago* (1963).

Another favourite of mine in the 'I never knew he played that' category was the title role in *One Day in the Life of Ivan Denisovich* (1970).

He was nominated for the Best Actor Oscar and the Golden Globe in *The Dresser* (1983), winning the latter. The Oscar nominations and the Golden Globe win are but two of many in the sphere of awards. Over his career there have been many notable performances that have met with critical acclaim. More recent film appearances were in *King of Thieves* (2018) alongside Michael Caine and Michael Gambon, among others, and the thoroughly charming *The Guernsey Literary and Potato Peel Pie Society* (2018).

In 2000 he published a much admired and acclaimed memoir, *Dear Tom: Letters from Home*. He was knighted in 2001 for services to cinema and theatre.

In *Football Fans* Tom regales us with recollections from his lifelong passion for following Hull City—The Tigers. I'm going to say that as a young boy he would never have imagined being the President of Hull City Supporters' Club, but that is precisely the position he holds with great pride and honour.

Memories of the Tigers

I first saw Hull City after the war in 1946 at the newly built Boothferry Park with my dad. I was born in February 1937, so I must have been nine years old. 0–0 it was, against local rivals Lincoln City. Tigers v Imps, Third Division North.

Memories are dim up until the arrival of Raich Carter as player-manager in 1948, though I can recall that we played Spurs in the fifth round of the FA Cup in 1954 when Alf Ramsey[1] was their full back. A draw at Boothferry Park in front of over 45,000, Spurs winning the replay at White Hart Lane. In the early 1950s we had a half back called Viggo Jensen who was Danish.[2] I can recall that Danish fishermen, as they left St Andrew's Dock to go the pub, used to give us pennies with holes in the middle. I was a fish dock lad.

We had a good Cup run under Raich Carter and Manchester United came to Hull in 1949 for a sixth round (quarter final) tie. I had only seen First Division[3]

1 Alf Ramsey would become more well known as a manager and led the England national team to World Cup victory in 1966.

2 Jensen had been spotted playing for Denmark and winning a bronze medal in the London Olympics of 1948. He went on to play over 300 games for Hull and scored 51 goals.

3 First Division would be the English Premier League today.

players on newsreels at the cinema and remember being surprised that, just like Hull City, they were flesh coloured. The ground was packed—kids sat on planks laid over bricks close to the edge of the grass. That wouldn't happen today, would it? United won 1–0—a controversial goal, obviously.

The 60s was a great time to be a City supporter. We had the fabulous strike partnership of Wagstaff and Chilton. Chilton was a local lad. Wagstaff came from Mansfield where he had been discovered by Raich Carter (managing The Stags at the time) who recommended him to our then chairman Harold Needler. Between them 'Waggie' and 'Chillo' scored a hatful of goals. They had to—our defence wasn't exactly watertight. My greatest memory during their era was a 1966 Cup match (a quarter final) against Chelsea, away at Stamford Bridge—within walking distance of my house in Fulham. My dad and I were sitting just in front of Richard Hutton, then playing cricket for Yorkshire (and later for England), and his father, the great Sir Leonard Hutton (arguably one of England's greatest batsmen). Imagine my dad's pride when we exchanged waves with our fellow Yorkshiremen. Not only that but we came back from 2 down, courtesy of two of Waggie's best efforts, to force a draw. My derisive Chelsea supporting pals were truly silenced.

When Chris Chilton became The Tigers' coach a match at Leyton Orient stayed long in my memory. With about 20 minutes to go we were 4–1 down but ended up winning 5–4. Memorable, eh? We had two players whom my wife Isabel called 'Big Billy' and 'Little Billy'. She said that Little Billy, aka Billy Askew, had sticky feet. Certainly, the left foot was 'sticky'. He had marvellous control with it. Big Billy, aka Billy Whitehurst, was more of a frightener. Talking of him once to Alan Hansen and Gary Lineker, I can remember them both going pale at the thought of having to mark Big Billy. He certainly had a profound effect on the poor lads of Leyton Orient that Saturday.

When Egyptian businessman Assem Allam became chairman of City he invited me to a party in honour of his fellow Egyptian (and my friend) Omar Sharif. Dr Allam had persuaded Hull University, to which he was very helpful, to give Omar a degree. When Omar and I worked together in the 60s he got interested through me in the Tigers' exploits. He remembered that Waggie had scored a lot of goals and was keen for him to come to the party. Which duly happened, to Waggie's great delight.

In 2014 we made it to the FA Cup final under manager Steve Bruce. It was against Arsenal. They'd be described as highflyers, I suppose. We made a good fist of it, losing 3–2 in extra time. Approaching the great stadium with Isabel before the game more than one City supporter said to us, *"Are we dreaming, Tom?"*

And now, as I write in September 2021, newly promoted to the Championship from League 1 and finding life hard, The Tigers are on television tomorrow against Sheffield United, newly demoted from the Premiership. And I will be glued.

Eric Knowles
(Burnley FC)—Antiques Expert

Football fans come in all shapes and sizes and from all sorts of backgrounds. There is no narrow template, so to speak, for football supporters.

Eric Knowles is one of those lovely people that provide the expertise on the BBC television program *The Antiques Roadshow*. In recent years he has also been one of the presenters of the spin-off show *Bargain Hunt*. Both shows are hugely popular in the United Kingdom and fondly admired by television viewers in Australia and many other countries.

Eric is an antiques expert in the decorative arts sphere and highly regarded for his knowledge of Moorcroft art pottery. Among Eric's *Antiques Roadshow* 'special finds' was when a lady turned up with a piece of glassware. In full *"How long have you had it, madam?"* mode, he discovered that it was *"bought in a car boot sale for a quid" and "had been stuck in the attic for years".* Eric immediately recognised it as a piece by the unrivalled glassmaker René Lalique but did not let on, of course! He has a warm, witty style that, to me, is only enhanced by the Lancashire accent forged in his hometown of Nelson in the county of the red rose. He also has a penchant for leading the *Antiques*

Roadshow customer along in a mischievous though polite way. And so it was with the Lalique vase. I still marvel at how he keeps himself in check whilst all the time knowing that this is a major find and from the miniscule purchase price builds up gradually to the staggering number of, *"Yes ... at least 20,000 pounds, madam."* Wonderful entertainment.

In 2001 the company that makes Moorcroft made him a non-executive director in recognition of his encyclopaedic knowledge. In addition to his own antiques business he also has a one-man show, *What Is It Worth?* that combines witty storytelling drawn from Eric's career along with audience members joining him on stage for a discussion of the heirlooms they have brought along.

In *Football Fans* Eric explains why he supports Burnley FC—his 'tribal team', as he described them when agreeing to contribute to the book.

The Turfites or the Clarets

My earliest interest in the 'Beautiful Game' was initially encouraged by my maternal grandfather who would take me to watch Nelson in what was then the Lancashire Combination. Complete with a second-hand blue-and-white scarf we headed across the Leeds and Liverpool canal, to the bottom of Carr Road, into the Seedhill football ground and into the equally second-hand all-wood stand.

It was here I learned the art of cheering on my team, belting out encouragement to my heroes at the top of my voice—my favourite being, *"Put some beef i'nt ball"*, much to my grandad's obvious embarrassment.

Truth be told, the encouragement was enhanced by the obligatory meat-and-potato pie plus a bottle of pop at half time, not forgetting the odd plastic soldier from the local market on the way home. Incidentally, Nelson FC[4] held

[4] Nelson FC currently play at Level Ten of English football, but in 1923 they had just won promotion from the Third Division (North). For season 1923/24 they were to be in the Second Division (what is now called The Championship). A pre-season tour of Spain saw victories over Real Oviedo (2–1) and Real Madrid (4–2). Their last year in the English Football League was in 1931.

the distinction of being the first English side to beat Real Madrid.

Meanwhile, my father was heading to nearby Burnley and Turf Moor where he was fortunate to watch that magical side that won the First Division title in the 1959–1960 season.

As much as I was devoted to Nelson FC, I soon became aware that Burnley FC were the bigger side that attracted gates of 30,000 or more, whilst their captain Jimmy Adamson had appeared on TV winning the ultimate accolade of Footballer of the Year in 1962. It took me another three years of cajoling and pestering my dad to take me on to 'The Turf'. Come 1963, he relented as by then I was now that bit taller.

My first game was when Blackpool were the visiting team and within seconds of arriving in the stadium it was only too apparent that I had arrived in what I recognised then as another world by virtue of the size of the crowd that dwarfed all I had known at Seedhill.

Here was a standing crowd of about 30,000 expectant souls packed shoulder to shoulder, many with arms and hands raised, grasping a claret-and-blue-painted rattle that collectively created an incredibly loud cacophony of noise that had me both transfixed and partially deaf for a short time. That noise increased by several decibels when the Burnley team emerged out of the tunnel and in less than two minutes my heroes were there before me, all of whom I could name as most had been part of the Division One Champions and the 1962 FA Cup side. I had watched that final at my grandad's house fully attired in my BFC strip—including boots.

Having lost 3–1 to Spurs that day, I feel no shame in admitting, as a soon-to-be totally devoted BFC nine-year-old, that I shed a few tears after the final whistle.

I soon realised that my father's reluctance to take me on 'The Turf' was well founded, as being of small stature, getting a decent view of the action proved a bit of an issue.

Ever the resourceful type of chap, my dear dad—then working as a joiner—made a folding tall wooden platform upon which I could stand and take in all the action. Never daunted, when my younger brother Bryan decided he wanted to share his newly found interest in football, our dad created a wider slide-on panel, enough to support both his sons, thus creating an alliance of three members of the Knowles clan sharing the same burning desire of a win—then worth two points.

Many years later, I remember watching a BBC TV comedy series known as *Ripping Yarns* starring a young Michael Palin who took on the role of Gordon Ottershaw in an episode titled 'Golden Gordon'. The episode featured the demise of Yorkshire team Barnstoneworth United. Set in 1935, the comedy depicts Gordon as the team's most devoted fan, and even has his son christened Barnstoneworth. Much to his father's pride, the somewhat nerdish child can recite the entire Yorkshire Premier League winning side of 1922. In truth, there is probably no shortage of both men and women of my vintage who might claim that same talent and offer the same when talking about the Burnley team of 1962. In goal Adam Blacklaw, in defence Alex Elder and John Angus, midfield Brian Miller, Jimmy Adamson (captain), Tommy Cummings, forwards John Connelly, Jimmy McIlroy, Ray Pointer, Gordon Harris and Jimmy Robson, not forgetting manager Harry Potts in the dugout.

For a town of less than 90,000 people, Burnley Football Club might still be respected for punching well above its weight. For decades, it has never been or wished to be recognised as being something of a 'glamour' club but is quite happy to settle to being something of a 'cult' club in a town where the town is the team, and the team is the town—but with fans from all parts of the UK and worldwide.

This is a real football club of a type that once reflected that of most teams in the football leagues at a time when football was very much a working man's game. This being prior to eventually being hijacked by big business and the money men—albeit those teams in the lower divisions have to manage and survive on often desperately lower gates and resultant incomes yet still command loyal support forever, to both my total amazement and respect.

Looking back to the team of '62, in the years that followed I was privileged to meet several players who will forever stay in my heart as immortal heroes.

Top of my personal hall of fame has to be Jimmy Adamson, who I met when still a boy and at, of all places, the Seedhill ground. It was during a game that featured a team of TV celebrities—I feel sure (multi-talented entertainer) Roy Castle was on one wing and (actor/singer) Jess Conrad the other. Jimmy A. was officiating as a linesman and just prior to the start of the second half I plucked up the courage to ask him for his autograph. Forever the gentleman, he told me that the game was about to start at any moment and to come back after the final whistle. I was seriously impressed that at the end of the match the great man turned around in an attempt to spot me, and I went home to proudly show my dad the much-prized signature in my autograph book.

Fast forward to 2000 and my invitation as a guest speaker to a celebratory dinner at Turf Moor to commemorate winning the 1960 First Division title and where many of the players involved were attending. I will never forget that loyal servant to Burnley, Brian Miller, tapping me on the shoulder to say thank you for all the occasions on TV and radio I was able to give the club a mention. It was one of the very few occasions that I felt a sense of fame—the fact that THE Brian Miller knew who I was. There was John Connelly, who way back sported a distinctive haircut that as a boy I was keen to emulate. Sadly, however, Mr C was now denuded on the follicle front. John eventually left Burnley to move on to Manchester United and was part of the England World Cup winning squad of 1966. Quite rightly; as the old films of his games for Manchester United show, he had a remarkable talent as the central motivator of his team. In later years, not only did he become the physical education teacher at my wife's school, but also set up a popular fish and chip shop aptly named *Connelly's Plaice*. Mindful that the late Tom Finney (one of England's greats), upon retiring from the game, returned to the plumbing trade, I ask myself if any of the overpaid prima donnas of today's beautiful game have given any thought to working in a fish and chip shop or as a plumber to keep up the payments servicing their fleet of Ferraris. I digress.

Jimmy McIlroy was the most mesmerising member of the team I was fortunate to watch, if only for one season before being sold by Burnley's controversial chairman Bob Lord to Stoke City in 1963. The following season Blackburn Rovers hosted the Stoke City side that featured the legendary Stanley Matthews but, equally important, also included 'Jimmy Mac'. As Burnley were playing away that Saturday my dad took me to the game where the number of claret-and-blue scarves almost outnumbered those of blue and white worn by the Rovers fans. Much to their consternation, and probably not mindful of the long-standing respect Jimmy Mac continued to enjoy from all Clarets fans.

Jimmy's contribution to Burnley has always been recognised by the Burnley faithful who regarded him with true affection, so much so that in Turf Moor today you can watch the game from the Jimmy McIlroy Stand.

Now, I must admit that my home outside London, plus my TV and other work schedules, limit my pilgrimages to Burnley. In years past the club kindly offered me tickets in the Bob Lord Stand for both me and my sons or my late father-in-law—who incidentally was at the 1962 Wembley final. We always appeared to find ourselves seated in the same area where, come half time, I soon recognised Jimmy some four rows below us and heading for a cup of tea. I am usually never shy in coming forward so don't ask me why it took me the best part of five years to introduce myself to the great man, but eventually I managed to pluck up courage when I saw him in the bar. What followed was a conversation still hard-wired in my brain during which he related episodes from his career. His endearing demeanour was punctuated by admitting that his favourite away game was Arsenal at Highbury where, he told me, you could always guarantee a massive crowd and that he *"loved to show off in front of them"*—his words not mine. I don't normally have time for show-offs, but I was more than happy to make Jimmy Mac my one exception, he being a true gentleman—and as you know, it takes one to know one!

Up The Clarets!

Ken Loach
(Bath City FC)—Film Director

Ken Loach is in the pantheon of film directors, one of only a handful of directors to win the Palme d'Or twice at the Cannes Film Festival. His awards were for *The Wind That Shakes the Barley* (2002) and *I, Daniel Blake* (2017). He is among the most successful of film directors in the various Cannes award categories, and his films have won multiple awards at other leading festivals. He has always worked closely with writers and believes that making a film is a team effort. And, as in football, there is no 'I' in the word 'team'.

Signature elements in his films are strong personalities and searing social critique. He established his reputation for hard-hitting film and TV drama in the 1960s on the BBC. My memory goes back to *Up the Junction*, *Cathy Come Home* and *Poor Cow* as being classical examples of his work in that era. They addressed issues of homelessness, low-income social housing, abuse and violence towards women—and note, this was well over 50 years ago. Likewise *Riff Raff* (1992), which examines employer malpractice and poor industrial safety in the construction industry.

My personal favourite is *Kes* (1969) from the book *A Kestrel for a Knave* by

Barry Hines, about a young boy from the north of England in a very poor home situation who finds solace in the training of a kestrel. It is full of incisive commentary and observation of a particular social environment and the 60s era in which it is set. It includes a brilliant football scene. Actor Brian Glover plays the role of the old-style school physical education teacher. It's all about his football prowess and winning (choosing the best players for his team in PE lessons) and his replica kit, rather than the health, well-being and enjoyment of the schoolboys. Wearing the red of Manchester United and a Number 9 on his back, he berates a boy for not knowing who he is: *"I thought you were Denis Law, sir?" "Don't you know your kits, lad, and your numbers? I'm Bobby Charlton this week—Denis Law's in the wash"*.

After service in the Royal Air Force, Ken read law at Oxford University, graduating in 1960. It was at Oxford that his future career was to take shape, directing and acting in theatre productions. In the early stages he worked in regional theatre and later joined the BBC as a director, most notably in his work for the seminal *Wednesday Play* series.

In *Football Fans,* Ken reveals his passion for Bath City, a club that plays in the sixth tier National League of English football and uses this context to develop a commentary on community ownership of football clubs.

Community-Owned Football Clubs

Football clubs can embody the communities where they play. Traditionally, the clubs are situated in the heart of working-class districts. Football has always been a working-class sport, the game on Saturday being a few hours respite from the daily routine. Many of the most famous clubs are in areas where life has been hardest, marked by poverty, low wages, and the struggle to act collectively for job security, better pay and working conditions. Solidarity has always been a prized virtue.

It was natural that this sense of loyalty should transfer to the football teams. The players represent us. Their victories are our victories, and when they lose, we all feel the pain. But unlike most losses, there is always another game next Saturday, and we live in hope that the sun will shine again.

What a contradiction it has been then, that these emblems of our communities should not belong to the people who live there but to a few businessmen. The largest clubs are now owned by international corporations or men of unimaginable wealth. Smaller clubs may have local owners, often with benign intentions who risk their own maybe limited funds. But the relationship to the supporters reflects the world beyond—a few own and control, while the many faithful followers and supporters remain powerless.

Hence the demand for community ownership. It seems obvious, doesn't it? The club can also grow in other ways. As well as being a place for football, it can become a centre for community activity, everything from being somewhere to meet, to providing training sessions for schools, to a venue for social gatherings. 'The club's the hub' is the slogan. It is a strong image and a fine aspiration.

The local team I now support is Bath City. It is semi-professional, playing way down in the sixth tier, but the passion and commitment at this level are as great as if we were playing in the Premier League. And a few years ago we became partly owned by local people and supporters who bought community shares. We now have a majority of shareholder votes.

It has been marked by some success on and off the field and attendances have nearly doubled. Thanks to an imaginative general manager, there's a real buzz around the ground on match days. The coach has encouraged an attractive style of football and the enthusiasm is infectious. The club's presence locally is becoming stronger. So far, so good. But the club is hampered by a long-standing debt, and there is no wealthy owner to pay it. Community-owned clubs must balance the books, with no safety net if they fail.

Like many clubs, Bath City has a charity attached, a foundation, to support local people and good causes. Since the change in ownership, it has developed its work extensively. One project that caught my eye was a film made by older people that recorded their memories of train journeys of their youth. Simple idea, but a source of pleasure and pride.

One problem emerges. Those who take positions of leadership within the new structure tend to have experience in business. Inevitably, that is a culture where managers take decisions and others carry them out. This can be at odds in an organisation which is founded on the principles of democracy and collectivism. The old consciousness where leaders lead and the rest are led resurfaces. Many supporters, used to the autocracy of the old ways, sink back into thinking that the board of directors takes decisions and we just go to the games and grumble.

A change of ownership is a necessary beginning, but it must be followed by a change of consciousness. We are not used to being active participants in decision-making. We tend to take what is given and complain; we must learn how to be democrats. When ownership passes to supporters and the community, we must all accept the responsibilities that accompany the new situation. There is no boss; we are the masters now!

Lex Marinos OAM (Panathinaikos FC)—Actor and Director

Lex Marinos is the performing arts 'everyman'. He is a film and television actor and director, a stand-up comedian, writer and radio presenter.

A keen follower of football but growing up in Wagga Wagga in the 1950s he also developed a fondness for rugby league and cricket.

Both his parents are of a Greek background, his father having migrated from Greece. Through his Greek-Australian mother he can trace convict ancestry in Tasmania!

In television, he has appeared in many widely admired drama series such as *Water Rats*, *A Country Practice* and *Rake*. As an actor he will be best known to many for his continuing role as Bruno in the long-running series *Kingswood Country*. Particularly notable work as a director is with the film *Indecent Obsession* and the TV mini-series *Bodyline*, the latter being a highly regarded dramatisation of the events associated with the Ashes tour of Australia by the England cricket team in 1932/33. This was broadcast in the United Kingdom by the BBC and by Network 10 in Australia. In 2012 he was a member of the award-winning cast for the ABC television mini-series *The Slap*.

Lex has taken up roles as both a producer and director of arts festivals around

Australia and served on the Australia Council (the forerunner to the Australia Council for the Arts). He was a member of the team that created and produced the Opening Ceremony of the 2000 Olympic Games in Sydney.

In his public speaking engagements Lex has carried a broad portfolio covering arts, cultural policy, immigration and sport. In 2008, he delivered the tenth annual Tom Brock Lecture (an annual scholarly lecture under the auspices of the Australian Society for Sports History where speakers focus on the history of rugby league football).

In 1994, he was awarded the Medal of the Order of Australia (OAM) for his services to the performing arts.

His book *Blood and Circuses: An Irresponsible Memoir* was published in 2014.

In *Football Fans* Lex explores his Greek heritage, waxing lyrical on one of the country's great clubs Panathinaikos and their rivalry with Olympiakos.

Derby of the Eternal Enemies

"Mother died STOP funeral Friday STOP Panathinaikos two Olympiakos one." This was the punchline to a joke my father used to tell about a villager breaking the bad, and good, news to his son in another village in the days when telephones were a rarity, and telegrams were the customary means of communication for urgent news. You were charged on the number of words, with the minimum being eight. Once the father had relayed the tragic news to his son, he found that he had only used half his allotted words, so he used the other half to convey the next most important news.

I have since discovered that this joke exists in many languages, wherever football is played, and local derbies dominate the lives of football supporters. Such rivalries are the lifeblood of football competitions around the world. Whether it be Manchester United vs Liverpool, Celtic vs Rangers, Boca Juniors vs River Plate, Real Madrid v Barcelona, Roma vs Lazio, the list is long. These are the games that thrill, make the heart beat a little faster and the blood flow a little hotter.

In Greece, the fiercest rivals are Panathinaikos and Olympiakos, and their contests carry the suitably Homeric label of 'Derby of the Eternal Enemies'. So dramatic, so epic, so Greek. Indeed, they are treated with awe and reverence, as though they were actual chapters from *The Iliad* or *The Odyssey*.

So, who are these Titans?

Panathinaikos was created in 1908 (under a slightly different name) to compete in a newly formed competition, nominally national, but in reality, a competition of clubs from Athens and surrounds. This competition was the forerunner of the current Super League Greece. Like most countries, including Australia, the competition passed through numerous iterations and formations before attaining its status.

Panath has won many championships and cups, several times securing the double, including a season undefeated, and have never been relegated from the top division. Under the management of the legendary Hungarian maestro, Ferenc Puskás, they are the only Greek club to have made the final of the European Club Championship (today referred to as the UEFA Champions League) in 1971, losing 0–2 to Ajax Amsterdam. The club's supporters are generally characterised as older, conservative, upper middle-class Athenians.

Olympiakos was founded in 1925, in the wake of the Asia Minor Catastrophe, which saw thousands and thousands of refugees repatriated to Greece, mostly settling in and around the port city of Piraeus. They brought with them mournful music, *rembetika* (a kind of Greek blues), hashish and staunchly working-class radicalism. It pains me to concede it, but their club is the most successful in Greece, winning countless championships, cups, doubles, and several astonishing runs of five or more consecutive titles. An obvious antagonist for Panath, politically and socially.

Australian summer is synonymous with swimming, cricket and tennis. But for the Greek expat community, as with other European diasporas, it also meant football. Football from 'home'. That is when I first became aware of these 'eternal enemies', as a young boy in the 1950s, growing up in Wagga Wagga, part of regional New South Wales.

At that time there was quite a strong Greek community in Wagga, many of them, like us, café owners. Communication was rudimentary in those days, impossible to comprehend in this immediately accessible, digital age. It usually involved booking an expensive three-minute international trunk call through the local telephone exchange. From late Saturday night or the early hours of Sunday morning the results would be relayed by a relative in Greece. I think there was a roster system. When it was Dad's turn to call it was to one of his brothers, Panayiotis or Yiorgos. Needless to say, despite Mum's anxiety, the expensive call usually exceeded its three-minute limit, whereupon the operator would cut in to ask whether he wanted another three minutes at some exorbitant rate. Of course, if it was a derby round, the call could account for a day's takings.

Sunday mornings involved relaying the scores around the community, which usually met socially on Sunday evenings when the cafes closed early. Then the discussion would really begin. I remember sitting at the table with the men. Most of them had Anglicised names by then, either voluntarily or otherwise. For instance, my father, Fotios Marinopoulos, had become Frank Marinos. He was joined by the owners of the Silver Key café, Nick and Steve Criticos (I don't know whether this was their 'real' name or whether they just identified as being Cretan); Peter Glekis from the Rose Marie; Andrew Soulis (White Rose); Sam Nomarhas (Capitol Theatre) and his nephew Harry; Xenephon Stathis (Popular); Mark and Sam Zouroudis; Alec Cook and Jack Williams and Jack Mitchell; young Andrew Theodore and Arthur Pappas who worked in our Bridge café. Then there was Con Poulos from the Georgian. He and Dad were as thick as thieves, not that they really were thieves, but if anything went missing or fell off the back of a truck, it usually turned up with Con or Dad.

They were the pre-World War II generation of migrants, youths and young men fleeing an impoverished, fragmented Greece, seeking a better life with opportunities to make money, which could be repatriated to needy families. Most followed friends or relatives into the catering trades. Future generations of Greek Australians (especially the post-World War II migrants) wryly referred to them as 'the milk bar aristocracy'.

They were anything but aristocratic, largely uneducated, and certainly nothing like the stereotypical Panath supporter. Nevertheless, Panath was their team.

It was a team that usually won, and Sunday evenings were full of satisfaction and merriment, much backslapping and lauding the feats of their club. It was as if they had personally influenced the result simply by the power of their support, divined from the other side of the world.

Losses were another matter. Any loss made the men morose and irritable, lackadaisically engaging in the festivities with the women and children. But this sense of melancholia was heightened when losing the derby, which seemed to happen far too regularly for anyone's liking.

I was amazed at how passionate they were, how forensically they were able to discuss a game they hadn't seen, and about which they knew little more than the result. They seemed to know about squandered chances, passes that missed their mark, shots that hit the woodwork, tackles that were ineffective, poor decisions. Especially from the referee. Con seemed to be a repository of esoterica. He remembered the referee from when they were at school together! Dubious, since at other times he would proudly proclaim he'd never been to school. This seemed closer to the truth.

Anyway, Con knew the referee; knew that his wife's cousin was married to the Olympiakos striker; knew that an Olympiakos official was blackmailing him for marital infidelity; knew that parcels of drachmas were being delivered to his house. Con knew the postman, went to school with him.

Incidentally, for a long time I thought there was only one referee, whose name was 'Pousti Malaka'. I soon learned that it was in fact a homophobic pejorative, levelled at any official who makes an adjudication against 'us'. It has resounded across the decades, from the earliest days of Pan-Hellenic in local competitions and then the National Soccer League. Even now in the A-League, you can identify the Greek supporters of various clubs the moment a controversial decision is made. Out comes the shouted epithet, passed on from generation to generation.

However, the Sunday evening analysis was not the end of it. In those days, there were a couple of weekly Greek-Australian newspapers, and they also carried results from Greece and sometimes a summary, enough to reignite the discussion. Phones would ring, opinions would be adamantly shouted down the line, so vehemently and loudly that it was questionable whether the phone itself was necessary or just a stage prop. Inevitably, Pousti Malaka was mentioned, daubed with vitriol.

It seems even more bizarre now than it did then, that these grievances would be given another airing some weeks later when newspapers from Greece would arrive via surface mail, often accompanied by a relative's eyewitness account. The phones would run hot again, hasty visits would be arranged, and the derby would be replayed at the back table of the café, over cigarettes, coffee and curses.

And so, as a boy, I learned the importance of rivalry, of derbies, across all codes of football, across sport in general. From matches between Pan-Hellenic (later Sydney Olympic) and Marconi, to Sydney FC and Melbourne Victory (Battle of the Blues) or Western Sydney Wanderers. My passion extends to Bledisloe Cup games where the All Blacks perennially resemble invincible Olympiakos and the Wallabies are like gallant but forlorn Panathinaikos. State of Origin rugby league, Ashes cricket, Olympic swimmers competing against USA, I watch them all, still imbued with the sense of awe and anticipation of that little boy in Wagga Wagga so many years ago.

All these contests engender heightened emotions of elation and despair through their inexorable narrative of heroism, triumph and tragedy. They transcend football and are invariably imbued with social overlays of class, politics and religion. They are tribal, and by supporting our club(s), we satisfy our own primal need to belong, to strive, to dream. They also teach us resilience in defeat, humility in victory. On a personal level, they help us (me) battle our (my) own eternal enemies.

Sir Tim Rice
(Sunderland AFC)—Lyricist

Tim Rice has worked in music, theatre and films since 1965 when he met Andrew Lloyd Webber, a fellow struggling songwriter. Rather than pursue Tim's ambitions to write rock or pop songs they turned their attention to Andrew's obsession—musical theatre. Their first collaboration, *The Likes of Us,* was based on the life of Dr Thomas Barnardo, the Victorian philanthropist. Their next three works together were much more successful—*Joseph and the Amazing Technicolor Dreamcoat, Jesus Christ Superstar* and *Evita.*

Tim has since worked with other distinguished popular composers such as Elton John (*The Lion King, Aida*), Alan Menken (*Aladdin, King David, Beauty and the Beast*), Bjorn Ulvaeus and Benny Andersson (*Chess*), and Stuart Brayson (*From Here to Eternity*). He has also written with Freddie Mercury, Burt Bacharach and Rick Wakeman, among others.

He is currently writing and presenting short weekly podcast chats (entitled *Get Onto My Cloud*) reminiscing about his years in music, theatre and film—playing hits and flops, out-takes and number ones. By March 2022 he had released over 60 episodes.

His recent musical *From Here to Eternity* is scheduled for a return to London in late 2022. A new production of the Tony-winning Broadway hit *Aida* (which has still not been seen in the West End) and a new Broadway presentation of *Chess* are also in the imminent works.

Sir Tim founded his own cricket team in 1973, which has now played over 700 matches. He was President of MCC (founded 1789) in 2002. Sir Tim was also appointed President of the London Library in 2017 in succession to Sir Tom Stoppard. He is a trustee of Sunderland AFC's Foundation of Light and a life vice president of the schools' cricket charity Chance to Shine. He crops up here and there in all branches of the media, drawing on his extensive knowledge of the history of popular music since Elvis was a lad. He has won several awards, mainly for the wrong thing or for simply turning up.

Sunderland AFC

I became a supporter of Sunderland Association Football Club in 1954, around the time of my tenth birthday. Sunderland were then flying high in the old First Division; they wound up fourth at the end of the 1954–55 season, level on points (48) with Wolves and Portsmouth but with an inferior goal average, a mere four points behind champions Chelsea.

Nearly all my chums at school back then supported local teams Luton Town or Watford. One or two expressed some enthusiasm for London sides such as Arsenal or Tottenham, or even the new champions, Chelsea. At least all these clubs were within a plausible distance from Hatfield, Hertfordshire, where I grew up. Casting my juvenile eye down the League Table, I decided to follow a team that no-one else in my class did. Sunderland, a place I knew nothing about, caught my eye—a romantic-sounding name that conjured up visions of sun and mystery. Furthermore, they were way ahead of Luton and Watford who were not even in the top flight.

However, I soon discovered that, with the exception of Newcastle United a few further miles up the road, I could not have selected a team further away from leafy Herts. But the die was cast—it was too late to change after expressing my undying loyalty to Sunderland for several weeks. Besides, they were challenging for the title.

That was the last time they seriously did so. I first saw them play in 1956 down south against Luton when they were hammered 6–2 but my devotion never wavered. I never saw them play at home until the glorious 1972/73 season when I went to Roker for the first time and was overjoyed to see them get revenge against the Hatters some 16 years later. And of course, they went on to win the Cup in the days when the Cup really mattered.

They still really matter to me.

The Clerics

Pope Francis
(San Lorenzo de Almagro FC)— Leader of the Roman Catholic Church

Cardinal Jorge Mario Bergoglio was elected pope in 2013 after the resignation of Pope Benedict XVI. He took the name Francis in honour of Saint Francis of Assisi. His papacy marked several firsts. The first Jesuit to become pope, the first from the Southern Hemisphere and the first from the Americas.

He was born in 1936 and has Italian heritage on both his father and mother's side. His father's family were migrants from Italy—leaving in the late 1920s to escape the fascist rule of Mussolini.

After graduating from a technical secondary school, he worked as a laboratory technician chemist in the food section of a scientific research company. Here he worked alongside Esther Balestrino, a left-wing activist who was a leading figure in the Mothers of the Plaza de Mayo movement.

He commenced studies at the seminary at the age of 19, entered the Society of Jesus at 21 and became a Jesuit officially at 23. After completing his studies at the seminary he taught literature and psychology in high schools. His theological studies commenced in 1967 when he was 31 and he was ordained to the priesthood just before his 33rd birthday. Following a distinguished career in various roles in the church he was created a cardinal in 2001 by Pope John Paul II. As pope he chooses to live in the Saint Martha guesthouse rather than the papal apartments. It is a guesthouse for Vatican officials, distinguished guests, visiting clergy and lay people of all faiths.

As well as football Pope Francis had a keen interest in tango dancing as a young man. He is also a fan of Argentinian movies and music.

Pope Francis is a keen football fan and visiting heads of state find it easy to choose a suitable gift for him—he is reputed to have an extensive collection of personalised team jerseys. In *Football Fans* he tells how he has been a lifelong supporter of San Lorenzo de Almagro FC from his home neighbourhood in Buenos Aires. In addition, he discusses the wider benefits of sport—the spiritual and mental as well as the physical. In response to my invitation to contribute to *Football Fans* he suggested that I use what he calls his 'Lay Encyclical' on sports. It is in the form of an interview reported in the famous sports newspaper *La Gazetta dello Sport.*[5]

Pope Francis's Lay Encyclical on Sport

The original interview was conducted and reported by Pier Bergonzi, Deputy Director of *La Gazzetta dello Sport.* January 2, 2021—Milan

Pope Francis: "My sport is rag ball. Being a goalkeeper has been a school of life"

Holy Father, you said that as a child you went to the stadium with your parents to watch football matches.

"I remember very well and with pleasure when, as a child, I used to go to the stadium with my family, it was known as The Gasometer. I particularly remember the 1946 championship, the one that my San Lorenzo won. I remember those days spent watching the players play and the happiness of us children when we returned home: the joy, the happiness on our faces, the adrenaline in our blood.

---

5 The article was published in January 2021 and is reproduced by kind permission of La Gazetta Dello Sport. It is translated from the original Italian.

Then I have another memory, that of the rag ball, (in Italian *pallone di stracci*; in Spanish *pelota de trapo*[6]). Leather was expensive and we were poor, and the rubber or plastic ball was not at all common, but a ball of rags was enough for us to have fun and almost work miracles playing in the little square near our house. As a child I liked football, but I wasn't among the best, on the contrary, I was the one who was, as we say in Argentina a *poto dura*, literally 'hard leg'. (Ed: Very honest appraisal by the Holy Father. In the modern vernacular I think we say: '*First touch? Hmmm—not so good*'.) That's why they always made me play in goal. But being a goalkeeper was a great life school for me. The goalkeeper must be ready to respond to dangers that can come from anywhere. And I also played basketball, I liked basketball because my dad was a pillar of the San Lorenzo basketball team."

Sport is also a party and a celebration. A sort of liturgy, of rituals, of belonging. It's not for nothing that we talk about *sporting faith*.

"Sport is all of what we have said: effort, motivation, development of society, assimilation of the rules. And then it is fun: I am thinking of the choreographies in football stadiums, of the writing on the ground when the cyclists pass, to the banners of encouragement when a competition is taking place. Trumpets, rockets, drums, as if everything disappeared, the world hung on that instant. Sport, when lived well, gives one celebration: we meet, we rejoice, we cry, we feel we 'belong' to a team. 'Belonging' and admitting that being alone it is not so nice—better to live, rejoice and party together. And curious, then, that someone connects the memory of something with sport: 'The year in which the team won the Scudetto; the year in which the champion won the competition. The year of the Olympics, of the World Cup'. In some way people's experience of sport and their passions, marks the personal and collective memory. Perhaps it is precisely these elements that authorize us to speak of 'sporting faith'."

---

[6] The notable award-winning feature film *Pelota de Trapo* was released in Argentina in 1948.

Is there a sports page, or an event, that you remember with pleasure?

"I don't have such great knowledge on the subject, but I can tell you that I follow all of them with interest. Sports stories that are not ends in themselves, but of people who try to leave the world a little better than when they found it. When, during an apostolic journey, I went to Yad Vashem in Jerusalem, I remember that I was told about Gino Bartali, the legendary Italian cyclist who, recruited by Cardinal Elia Dalla Costa, and appearing to be on a training run on his bike, he left Florence for Assisi and returned with dozens of false documents hidden in the frame of the bicycle. These were used by Jews thus enabling them to flee and be saved. He cycled hundreds of kilometres every day knowing that, if he was stopped, it would be the end of him. His actions offered a new life to entire families persecuted by the Nazis, even hiding some of them at his house. It is said that he helped save about 800 Jews and their families during the barbarism to which they were subjected. He said that good is done and not said, otherwise what good does it do? Yad Vashem considers him 'Righteous Among the Nations', recognizing his commitment. Here is the story of a sportsman who left the world a little better than he found it."

Defeat and victory are part of sporting dynamics, like the fact of living.

"Winning and losing are two verbs that seem to oppose each other: everyone likes to win and nobody likes to lose. Victory contains a thrill that is even difficult to describe but defeat also has something wonderful. For those who are used to winning, the temptation to feel invincible and strong: victory, sometimes, can make you arrogant and lead to think you have made it. Defeat, on the other hand, favours meditation: wondering why you have lost is an examination of conscience, the work done is analysed. That is why, from certain defeats, beautiful victories are born: because, once the mistake has been identified, the thirst for redemption is ignited. I would say that those who win do not know what they lose. It's not just a play on words: ask the poor."

Behind every great champion there is a coach. Coaching is a bit like educating?

"In some ways yes. When an athlete wins, their coach is almost never seen: he doesn't go up on the podium, he doesn't wear the medal, the cameras rarely frame him. And yet, without a coach, a champion is not born: you need someone who 'bets' on him, who invests time, who knows how to glimpse possibilities that not even the athlete would imagine. That is a bit visionary, I dare say. Forgiveness, it's not enough to train your body: you need to know how to speak to the heart, to motivate, to correct without humiliating. The more brilliant the athlete, the more delicate they are to handle: the true coach, the true educator, knows how to speak to the heart of those who are born champions. Then, in the moment of the competition, they know how to step aside: they accept that they must depend on the athlete. The athlete will come back in case of defeat to face up to it."

Can a healthy competitive spirit also help the spirit to mature?

"Two passages written by Saint Paul in his letters come to mind. The first: 'Don't you know that, in races in the stadium, everyone runs, but only one wins the prize? Run yourselves too in order to win it' (1 Corinthians 9:24). It is a beautiful invitation to get involved, so as not to look at the world from the window. The second passage that I would like to recall is when Paul, speaking to his friend Philemon, gives as if confiding his secret to him: 'I run because I want to reach the prize' (Philippians 3:12). No athlete runs just to run: There is always some beauty which, like a magnet, draws one who undertakes a challenge to himself. It begins always because there is something that fascinates us."

The heart is at the centre of sporting activity as well as religious experience. Keeping it 'trained' is the secret to not losing talent?

"Keeping the heart in order is the secret for any victory, not just for sports: the psalmist, in fact, asks God: 'Let my heart be whole' (Psalm 119.80). If we look at the history of talent, we realize that so many talented people got lost precisely because of disorder. An orderly heart gives a happy heart, a state of grace, ready for the challenge. I think that if we asked any athlete the ultimate secret of their victories, more than anyone would tell us, is that they win because they are happy. Happiness, therefore, is the consequence of an orderly heart. A happiness to share because if I keep it to myself, it remains a seed, if instead I share it, it can become a flower."

Many champions tell of having begun their sporting adventure in the shadow of a bell tower, in the 'field of the oratory' of a church in the city centre or in the extreme suburbs.

"The Church has always had a great interest in the world of sport. We can say that in sport the Christian communities have identified one of the most understandable grammars to speak to young people.

Let us think of Don Bosco and the Salesian oratories but let us think of all the parishes in the world, including especially the poorest, in which there is always a field available to play and play sports. Through the practice of sport, a young person is encouraged to give the best of himself, to set himself a goal to achieve, not to be discouraged, to collaborate in a group. And a wonderful opportunity to share the pleasure of victory, the bitterness of a defeat, to get together and give the best of oneself."

You, as a Jesuit, and spiritual and cultural son of Saint Ignatius of Loyola, 'champion' of the Exercises Spiritual. 'Exercise' is synonymous with training. Is there any relationship between sport and the exercises of St. Ignatius?

"When St. Ignatius of Loyola wrote the Spiritual Exercises, he did so by thinking back to his history as a soldier, made up of exercises, training, training. It senses that the spirit, like the body, must also be trained. Practicing, then, requires discipline: the exercises are good teachers. Guillaume de Saint-Thierry, a Belgian monk who lived in the twelfth century, says that 'the will generates practice, practice generates exercise, and exercise procures strength for any work.' The exercise of goodness, beauty, truth are occasions in which man can discover unexpected resources within himself. And then play with them."

What type of sportsman do you appreciate the most?

"Thank you for not letting me name your own: it is unpleasant to choose one at the expense of the other. I appreciate, however, those who are aware of the responsibility of their talent, whatever sport or discipline they belong to. The 'champion' becomes, inevitably, a model of inspiration for others, a sort of muse, a landmark. It is important that athletes and champions are aware of how much their words, their attitude, affects thousands of people. There are very beautiful aspects: I think, and I take this opportunity to thank them, of the boys of the Italian national football team who every year with their coach, go bed by bed, to visit the children in the pope's hospital (The Bambino Gesu Children's Hospital), first of all in the oncology ward. This also happens for other hospitals and in many countries. A way to realize the dreams of children who suffer. When, however, the champion forgets this dimension, he loses the beauty of being such, the opportunity to make sure that those who take them as a model can improve, grow, also become a champion too. I wish the champions to learn a precious virtue: temperance, the ability not to lose a sense of proportion. Only in this way will they be able to witness the great values such as honesty, fairness, dedication. These are not trivial things."

Football, or rather sport, has recently mourned the death of Maradona, considered by many to be the greatest footballer ever. What did he represent for your Argentina?

"I met Diego Armando Maradona during a match for Peace in 2014: I remember with pleasure everything Diego did for the Scholas Occurrentes, the Foundation that takes care of the needy all over the world. On the pitch he was a poet, a great champion who gave joy to millions of people, in

Argentina as in Naples. He was also a very fragile man. I have a personal memory linked to the 1986 World Cup, the one that Argentina won thanks to Maradona. I was in Frankfurt, it was a difficult time for me, I was studying the language and collecting material for my thesis. I had not been able to see the final of the World Cup and I only knew the day after the success of Argentina on Germany, when a Japanese girl wrote on the blackboard 'Viva I' Argentina' during a German lesson. I remember it, personally, as the victory of solitude because I had no-one with whom to share the joy of that sporting victory: loneliness makes you feel alone, while what makes joy beautiful is being able to share it. When I was told of Maradona's death, I prayed for him and sent the family a rosary with a few words of comfort."

The Vatican City has its own athletics team. Then there is the 'Clericus Cup', a sort of championship for the students of the pontifical universities. It's not just sports.

"Evangelising means witnessing, in personal and in community life, to the life of God in us, the one that was given to us in Baptism. There are no strategies, there is no sense in marketing faith: only when a man or a woman sees a man or a woman living like Jesus, then they can be fascinated and will be able to begin to take seriously the proposal of the Gospel. It is evangelised with the fascination of one's own life that has the taste and taste of the Beatitudes. The athletics teams and the Clericus Cup find the meaning of their presence in the Vatican precisely to witness an evangelical style in sport. It is also a way to build community. I think of the variety of athletes who come from the administrations: Swiss Guards, gardeners, pharmacists, employees of the Vatican Museums, the Papal Villas, priests and perhaps even some monsignors. An outgoing Church ... on the sports fields!"

There is an Arabic proverb that says: "Don't give up. You would risk doing it an hour before the miracle." A proverb that faith and sport share.

"Your surrender is the dream of your opponent: surrender and let them win. And always a risk: "What if I had resisted a moment longer?", you will continue to tell yourself for who knows how many times seeing how it ended. Then it is also true that there are days when it is better to keep fighting, others when it is wiser to let it go.

Life is like a war: you can lose a battle, but not the war! A man does not die when he is defeated: he dies when he surrenders, when he ceases to fight. The poor, from this point of view, are a spectacular example of what it means not to give up. Not even in the face of the evidence of indifference: they continue to fight to defend their lives."

Bishop Libby Lane
(Manchester United FC)—
Church of England Lead Bishop for Sport

Libby Lane is the Bishop of Derby, a diocese in the English Midlands. She is the first woman to be consecrated as a bishop in the Church of England and sits in the House of Lords as one of the 26 Lords Spiritual.

Although born in Buckinghamshire she was raised in Derbyshire. High school was in Manchester, and she read theology at St Peter's College, Oxford, where she met her husband George, who is also an Anglican priest.

I want this book to show that the passion for football covers a wide spectrum of people. Bishop Libby's involvement is a vivid expression of this. When I contacted the Archbishop of Canterbury as a potential contributor to this book (he follows Sunderland AFC) he was very interested in the project and very encouraging. Whilst he wished me well, he recommended that Bishop Libby might be better placed as she is the Church of England's lead Bishop for Sport.

Before approaching Bishop Libby, I sought to determine whether she had any particular connection with football. From an interview being reported in *The Times* newspaper a few years ago I found this: *"... but supporting Manchester*

United and being alert to the football season is something I simply can't avoid ... it's in my DNA."

I thought, as we say in Australia, *"It sounds like we might be cooking with gas!"*

Bishop Libby was enthusiastic in agreeing to contribute to *Football Fans*. She did, though, set down parameters. She would only be willing to write if she was free to include the connection between her faith and her love for football and her desire to be lead Bishop for Sport in the C of E. Would I be content with her referencing her faith and beliefs in an appropriate way? Could I explain how I thought having her contribute a chapter would add value to the book, and how would her writing a chapter add value to her ministry as lead Bishop for Sport?

My answer was that for me those elements would appear to be the most important. In short, I replied, that for Bishop Libby to address the connection between her faith and her love for football is precisely what I would wish for. It was intrinsic to my rationale for inviting Bishop Libby to contribute. So that is what we get—football, faith and Manchester United.

Football, Faith and Manchester United

Supporting Manchester United is what we do in our family. No, it's deeper than that—being Man United supporters is who we are. It's been part of our DNA for four generations. My dad's a Mancunian born and bred, and he grew up watching Man U with his dad at the Maine Road Stadium—which they shared with Manchester City after the war (1946–49) while Old Trafford was repaired from bomb damage. It's hard to imagine such mutuality nowadays.

When I became the Church of England's first woman Bishop, the media picked up my love for Man United and MUTV (United's own TV channel) interviewed me. They asked which came first, faith or football. Chronologically that's an easy question—football, and Manchester United specifically, came first—part of life since before birth. Faith, I came to later, going to church on my own from the age of 11 after being invited to a church youth club in the neighbouring Derbyshire village from where I grew up.

In terms of priority that would be a harder question! Thankfully, I don't think I have to choose. Loving my team is part of who I am, and all of me is loved by God. I love God back with everything of me including being an avid sport fan.

During the Euros 2020 (in 2021 because of the COVID pandemic) I was interviewed by Radio 5 Live prior to the semi-finals in which England were to play Denmark. At the end of the interview, I was asked to pray for England (something they said was a first for 5 Live). I agreed but explained that I wouldn't be praying for a win as I don't think God is a lucky charm or has favourites. But I prayed and England won. So, I was asked back for a follow-up interview before the final. Of course, we lost that match on penalties. I was saddened that my prayer had not been fulfilled—not because I'd been praying for a win but because I'd been praying that the match would build goodwill and a sense of hope and shared identity, and, in fact, there was terrible racist abuse towards some of the England football team in the aftermath, including about Jadon Sancho and Marcus Rashford who played for Manchester United.

We are each and all responsible as those engaged in sport at every level for our own individual choices and behaviours and for the influence we bring to confront, challenge and change group behaviours. But organisations like the FA and major football teams in it have responsibilities too.

My general memories of going to Old Trafford as a teenager in the 1980s, sometimes with my dad who had season tickets and so designated seats and sometimes with my friends standing at the Stretford End, are wonderful—they were great occasions, of belonging and growing expectation. But there were times I was aware of singing, shouting, interaction that was offensive and intimidating, and occasionally violent. Much has been done to try to address those behaviours, and anti-racist campaigns, such as the Premier League's 'No Room for Racism', are now high profile and promoted by teams like Manchester United.

Sport can be such a power for good, but it is also a context with potential for real harm as we have seen in continuing examples of not only racism, but sexism and prejudice and discrimination against LGBTQ+ individuals and those with disabilities. It makes me angry when sport, which brings such joy to me and countless others, is used for hatred and abuse.

I am now the Church of England's lead Bishop for Sport, a new role that I'm shaping to reflect my own passion but also because I think sport matters. I support churches engaging in sport locally as a way to engage and enhance their local communities for the common good, and to share the Gospel; I support Sport Chaplaincies as they resource local and elite sport and all who work and play in that sector; and I engage through my role in parliament as a Lord Spiritual (in the House of Lords) recognising how significant all sport (including football) and physical health is economically and culturally, from grassroots to elite competition, for individual, community and national well-being, cohesion and inclusion. It's great to think that my dad sharing his love for football and passion for Manchester United had such influence for good on me that I now offer this role for church and country.

Football People

Steve Darby

(Devonport FC and The Matildas)—Professional Coach and Consultant

Steve Darby is a Merseysider who grew up following Liverpool. He played as a goalkeeper at school, youth level and later in Australia and the USA. He maintains that his career in the professional ranks was only limited, to quote Steve himself, by a severe lack of ability! However, there is no doubt that he has had a distinguished career as a coach. His piece in *Football Fans* recounts what brought him to Australia and led to him being enchanted by Devonport FC and then to coaching Australia's national women's team (as head coach from 1989 to 1991). He was a FIFA Instructor for Oceania and an Asian Football Confederation (AFC) coaching instructor. One of his roles with the Australian federation was as national youth development manager.

He left Australia in 1997 to coach in the Malaysian National League with Johor FA, winning promotion and the Malaysian FA Cup. He has also won a South East Asian Games gold medal in 2001 as coach with Vietnam. After a spell back in the UK coaching the youth team at Sheffield Wednesday, he coached Home United in Singapore, winning the FA Cup twice, the league, and reaching the AFC Cup semi-finals. In a later spell in Malaysia with Perak, he won the Super Cup and AFC Cup qualification. In 2008/9 he was the Thailand national team coach with two notable former England players as the national team manager—first with Peter Reid and then Bryan Robson. He has also had a successful stint in India coaching in the inaugural Indian Super League with Mumbai City FC. As Technical Director and National Coach of the Laos Football Federation for their 2018 World Cup Qualification program he took the country to their highest-ever FIFA ranking.

He now lives back in the UK where, drawing on his extensive experience in Asia, he works as a consultant and pundit with Asian media outlets. Steve's biography, *The Itinerant Coach*, was written by Antony Sutton and published by Fair Play Publishing in 2021.

Devonport

It was 1979, I had just passed my English Football Association 'Full Badge', apparently one of the youngest ever at 24, when I received a telegram (remember those?)! It was asking me if I wanted to be a player/coach in Tasmania. I thought, well, I'd always wanted to work in Africa, and I *had* passed my Geography 'A' level! I soon realised it was at the bottom of Australia and, in fact, the next stop would have been Antarctica – and not the African continent. I rang a cricketer mate who had played there, and he described it as the land of the ABC. A for apples, B for beer and I will let you guess the C!

So off I went on a gruelling 24-plus-hour flight and ended up at Launceston Airport. As well as the club directors, there was a lone journalist to meet me, showing me how important I was. He asked me if I could walk down the plane steps with a bag over my shoulder, juggling a ball. I suggested if I could do this, it would be Milan or Madrid airport.

As I always did, I bought a newspaper at the airport to try to gain local knowledge. Naturally, I went to the back page and saw the football results. Penguin: 86, Cooee: 79. I thought to myself, *I will be a decent 'keeper here!*

I soon discovered the game of men—and only men in those days—wearing sleeveless shirts and tight shorts and being able to punch each other without a red card. The game won me over eventually and I played and coached a few years later.

The club that brought me to Tasmania was Devonport, which was on the banks of the river Mersey—the other Mersey, of course. From the airport, the directors drove me directly to the club where they told me I was putting on a coaching session. It was a heck of a session as every club player was there. Five teams and a youth team all on one pitch.

In all seriousness, the club was and still is today a brilliant club. The directors supported me to the hilt and never interfered with selection. I didn't realise at the time how unusual that was and I certainly cherished it. The next big shock for me and the club was that they saw I was injured and were concerned as to when I would be able to take my place in midfield for the team. Apparently, the person who had spotted me on my Full Badge course thought I was a midfielder. I think being the youngest on the course just meant I had to do all the running!

The players were great and were shocked when I knew their names. I had asked for a team photo to be sent to me so I could learn quickly. I always had trouble saying Fabio Pizzerani, but Pete Best was a lot easier to remember!

Our first away game was a shock as we stopped the coach on the way to Hobart and the centre-back Alex McDonald went to the boot and let his pigeons out! That was a first to me and to be honest has never happened again.

The lads were great, dedicated, keen to learn and improve, and we had a good season. However, what impressed me most was that the club truly belonged to the community. It looked after primary schools, worked with charities, developed sponsorships and ran bingo sessions, which were packed. In fact, apparently, it was the bingo that paid my wages. Over the years the club has gone from strength to strength, winning many Tasmanian trophies, developing players and also developing facilities that are a credit to such a small city. As I write they have recently had another run in the Australia Cup representing Tasmania.

I still follow the club and, even though it was over 40 years ago, I am still in contact with a few players and officials, though a number of these players are now grandads. This epitomises what the club is. A true football club that belongs to the community. I was transient, a professional passing through, but I can still never forget the players and the committee who gave me a start in my Australian coaching career. That career was to last 17 years and involve five Tasmanian clubs, two Canberra clubs, the Sydney Olympic club in New South Wales and the national federation.

So, to Devonport, I thank you for helping me and for developing the real football in the heart of Aussie Rules. So, I thank Rimmer x2, Best, McDonald, Smith, Gleeson, Rigby, Frame, McKenna … and of course, Pizzerani! And the committee team of Rimmer, Mullett, Pattison and Haines.

The game will never die whilst there are clubs like this.

The Matildas

I first was invited to be involved with coaching the Australian national women's team in 1985; the nickname Matildas was not adopted until many years later. I had not coached a women's team before but whilst I had been Tasmanian Director of Coaching, I had encouraged women to take coaching courses as I saw that the future of the game lay in mums encouraging their children to play the game. I was a little sceptical at first, but the opportunity to visit Xian in China was too good to give up. Despite there being horror stories of that trip in 1984 to China, including rats the size of dogs and inedible food, I was won over by the quality and attitude of the players. Players such as the talented Dolan, the hard-as-nails Monteath, the Millman sisters and the 'Big Fella' up front, Isieref. Their willingness to work hard, never moan and their love for playing football opened my eyes to women's football.

I always believed football was for everyone. I never felt race, religion, gender or sexuality had any effect on loving the game and there were good and bad people from all aspects of that spectrum. This trip, however, opened my eyes to the quality of female players.

My next brief journey was to take the Australia Gold team (the 'B' team) to play in a four-team tournament (the Oceania Cup) in Brisbane in 1989. This tournament also included the Australian Green team which, in essence, was the national team. I soon discovered I had a wide range of players who had been chosen by the 'kitchen table' method of state-based selection. This did bring up some gems in the shape of Moya Dodd and Jane Oakley. Also, there was a tough Queensland mum in Michelle Sawyers, a technically excellent keeper in Kim Schaefer (daughter of Manfred, a well-known former Socceroo and coach in Australia) and a wild Italian striker with pace in Angela Iannotta. The current Junior Matildas coach, Raeanne Dower, was in that squad too. Many of these players would enter my first national team when I was appointed in 1989.

When I was appointed, the first thing I did was take the advice of Bill Shankly, my ultimate coaching hero. I picked the team, not a selection committee. Basically, a coach lives and dies on results, and if I was going to lose, it would be on my own decisions. So, I chose the team from the National Championships, and I listened to people I trusted in various locations who gave me recommendations. It makes me laugh when people compare coaching in Belgium or Holland to Australia. Geography is such a massive factor; in this case more so, as these players had to fund their own travel to central venues.

When I got the job, the first thing I did was watch the best female players in the world on video. In this case it meant players in the USA, Sweden, Norway and China. What stood out to me immediately was that these top players were athletes. If Australia was to compete, I had to choose the best footballers and the best athletes. I made what were a few surprise choices. I saw Gegenhuber punch Murray, who was the most skilful player. I saw Forman tackle superbly and see things very few others did. I saw Tann ooze leadership and dominance. Dodd was a good header of a ball with vision and Wheeler was a proper goalkeeper and was six feet tall. Schaefer was technically excellent but very small. The key was: could good footballers like Murray and Forman match the physical prowess of

Tann, Oakley and Gegenhuber? I needed players who could play the piano and players who could carry it!

The present-day Matildas are superbly supported by an excellent staff, but at that time there was only me, Andrew Young (a qualified physio), Dr Kieran Fallon, (a brilliant doctor) and Marie-Louise Agius as administrator. She was a bit like Radar in MASH. She knew everything I needed in advance and was a superb link between myself and the players.

Training camps and tours were few and far between in those days and, important to note, were player funded. There cannot be enough praise for the sacrifices these players made to their careers outside of football, their families and relationships, to have the honour of playing for Australia. That was the overriding theme—'Honour'. These players saw it as an honour to play for Australia. They never moaned about anything. They worked hard; in fact, most worked harder than male full-time players in the National Soccer League (NSL). These players would often train before and after work on their own. They were given individual training programs and were tested at the Australian Institute of Sport (AIS) whenever we could get access to that facility. Oakley and Gegenhuber smashed beep test records and Tann lifted weights that Mark Viduka was lifting at that time.

Football does create memories, such as Hughes and Tann playing in men's teams to get better. Once in a practice match vs the AIS a tough Forman sailed 'over the top' on Kevin Muscat. Not many are brave enough to do that. And as he squared up to her, about six of her teammates surrounded him.

There were good results and bad results, but the results are irrelevant now. These pioneers paved the way for the current Matildas to be getting the treatment and praise they deserve and, yes, the money! The saying is there are some things money can't buy—and the character of this group of players epitomises this.

Frank Farina OAM
(The Socceroos)—
Coach and Former Player

I've often found football to be an easy way into communicating with people when travelling overseas. Knowing who the local team is and maybe a notable player or two. It's a similar reaction to showing a willingness to exchange pleasantries, at least, in the local lingo—people warm to it. And so it was on a recent holiday in Puglia, Italy.

A middle-aged guy came to our accommodation to deliver water and so we had a bit of "*Buon giorno*" and "*Come va*" while the pump was whirring away. He wanted to know where we were from. Australia is Australia in Italian so no problem there. Add, "*Ti ricordi Franco Farina, giocatore di calcio,*" and we were friends for life!

Frank Farina was born in Darwin and grew up in Papua New Guinea and Far North Queensland. His father was an Italian migrant and his mother a Torres Strait Islander.

His is one of the distinguished names in Australian football—both as a player and a coach. For the first five years of his professional career, he played in

Canberra and Sydney, winning championships with Sydney City and Marconi, twice winning Player of the Year (the forerunner to the Warren Medal) and twice being leading goalscorer. He moved to Europe in 1988 and played in Belgium, Italy (with Bari in Puglia), France and briefly on loan in England.

He won the Belgian championship with Club Brugge in the 1989–90 season (33 appearances and the league's top scorer with 24 goals). He returned to Australia in 1995 and was player-coach of the Brisbane Strikers in 1996-97 when they won the championship. He played for Australia in several age group teams and played 67 games for 14 goals at senior international level, retiring from international competition – some would say prematurely – in 1995, aged 31.

He has coached at club level in Brisbane and Sydney. From 1999 to 2005 he was the coach of the Socceroos and has also coached the national teams of Fiji and Papua New Guinea.

Frank's record with the Australian national team stands comparison with any other coach—a win record of a tick over 58% in 'A' Internationals. Notable wins included Hungary in Budapest and over England in London (at West Ham's ground). In the 2001 Confederations Cup Frank's side beat France (the reigning World Cup holders) and, to take third place, Brazil, who were to win the World Cup the following year.

In 1998, he published his playing biography *My World Is Round* as told to Bonita Mersiades.

In 2000 he was awarded the Medal of the Order of Australia (OAM) for his services to soccer as a player and coach as well as the Centenary Medal. Professional Footballers Australia named him as winner of the Tobin Medal in 2009.

Australia—My Heart Bleeds Green and Gold

I wasn't 'born' into following a club.

The team that was my heritage on my dad's side was Bologna in Italy as that is where he was from. So as a small kid, I had this faint family attachment to far-away Bologna, which of course I never got to see on TV.

I started playing informally when I was seven in 1971, so by the time the 1974 World Cup rolled around with the Socceroos in it for the first time, I was as aware as any ten-year-old could be growing up in New Guinea and then Far North Queensland of some of the big-name players in the game.

Locally, it was Peter Wilson, Ray Baartz, Ray Richards, Johnny Warren, Harry Williams, Atti Abonyi and 'Noddy' Alston, to name a few.

Internationally, Bobby Moore, Franz Beckenbauer, Johan Cruyff, Gerd Müller, Gigi Riva, Dino Zoff, Eusébio were just some of the names of that time who resonated with me. Plus one George Best, the 470-game veteran of Manchester United and, as a Northern Irishman, one of the greatest players never to play in a World Cup.

My faint attachment to Bologna became a more-than-faint attachment to Manchester United in the 1970s and my support for United has continued since then.

However, if I am to say what is the team of my heart and my mind, it is the Socceroos.

I never dreamed of being a professional footballer. I played because I loved it and, especially when I started playing with my older brothers, most of all I really loved beating them. But from the beginnings of backyard football in Papua New Guinea, I moved on to club and school sport in Cairns from when I was ten years of age. By the time I was 16, I was playing for Mareeba in the State League, but it still didn't enter my mind I would play the game professionally. That finally dawned on me as a possibility in 1982 when I was selected to go to the second intake of football players at the Australian Institute of Sport in Canberra.

Things became serious. There would not be a professional player alive who wouldn't want to play for their national team—and when you're in a set-up like the AIS, you've not only got an expectation for yourself but the other players around you too.

Playing for the Young Socceroos at the 1983 World Cup was a huge thrill for a kid from regional Australia. Getting selected for the Socceroos by Frank Arok in 1984 as a 19-year-old was unbelievable. Between then and when I retired from international competition in 1995, I was never out of the team, other than due to suspension or injury.

Like many of the men I played with, I'll never be able to say, "I played in the World Cup", but I do see that it's because of those who came before me, my generation of players, and those who have come afterwards, that we are all part of making that dream a reality for the past five World Cup final tournaments.

I've watched and played in some wonderful football matches—and even scored in a few!—but nothing pulls at the football heartstrings more than watching Australia play in a World Cup finals tournament; even more so when we perform as well as we did in the 2022 tournament. I was so pleased for the players and for 'Arnie' (Graham Arnold) and his team, and so pleased for all those who support the Socceroos.

It was an incredible honour and privilege to be a Socceroo, as it was also to become coach of the team from 1999 to 2005, and to be the first Australian-born coach.

But before I ever played or coached, I was a passionate fan and supporter, and that never leaves you. I'm green and gold till I die.

Heather Garriock
(Heart of Midlothian)—Former Professional Player and Coach

When responding to my invitation to contribute to *Football Fans* writing about her favourite team, Heather answered, *"I'd love to, but I follow Hearts. It's my dad's fault—he's Scottish."* My answer was, *"What do you mean by 'but'?"*

As I explained to her, this book is not just about the big, glamorous teams. It's about the full, broad spectrum of football and the people who are passionate about it—big time, small time and everything in between. Sure, Daniel Craig (Mr Bond, as was) or Elvis Costello on Liverpool would be great but Heather Garriock, a distinguished international footballer for Australia, writing about her passion for Heart of Midlothian in the Scottish Premier League would be too.

Heather's senior playing career stretched across years 1996 (debuting at the age of 13) to 2014 with games at the top level in Australia, USA, Denmark and Sweden. She played 139 games for Australia's national women's team between 1999 and 2011 and scored 21 goals in the green and gold. She is Matilda No. 108. Tournament appearances include three senior World Cups (USA 2003, China 2007 and Germany 2011), three Asian Cups (Australia 2006, Vietnam

2008 and winning in China 2010), and two Olympic Games (Sydney 2000 and Greece 2004).

After her playing career she coached at Sydney University and at Canberra United in the 'W' League—forerunner of the 'A' League Women's.

She now works in sports administration. At the time of writing she is the CEO of Australian Taekwondo.

Heather is a director on the board of Football Australia. She won the Julie Dolan Medal (awarded to the player of the season in Australia) in 2002–03. She was inducted into the Football Australia Hall of Fame in January 2022, along with fellow Matilda Kate Gill, legendary Socceroos goalkeeper Mark Schwarzer and Huxley Honeysett, a stalwart of the development of the game in Tasmania.

... but I Follow Hearts

I know it sounds like a random choice, but in fact, I was born to be a Hearts fan. Or should I say, I was born a Hearts fan. Growing up in Australia in Western Sydney, my grandfather, who was in Edinburgh, used to send us VHS[7] tapes of Hearts games, and the 'Best 100 goals' from the Scottish Premier League. Every morning, religiously, with my younger brother Nathan, we'd get up before school and watch the tapes. We had two choices: Hearts highlights or the top 100 goals from the Scottish Prem. I learnt the Hearts song and I would be singing it while watching ... *Hearts, Hearts, glorious Hearts ...*

It inspired me to play football. I signed up for Leppington Lions in the local community league at age five. I wanted to play football like my dad. We would play outside in the backyard after school with my sister Vanessa, brother Nathan, and mates Michelle and David Carney (David would later play in Europe and for the Socceroos including at the 2010 World Cup finals in South Africa) and I'd mimic the players I saw on the video.

I fell in love with the game at such a young age because of the influence of

7 For younger readers VHS is an 'ancient' form of 'catch up'! Look up 'VHS' on Google

my Scottish father and grandfather. My great memory of being a Hearts fan was the 1998 Scottish Cup final at Celtic Park. Hearts beat Rangers 2–1. I vaguely remember Colin Cameron scoring a penalty early in the game and then Stéphane Adam scoring the winning goal. Nothing better than the 'Jam Tarts' beating Rangers.

I was in Scotland in 2003 and had the most fantastic experience. As part of the Matildas pre-World Cup tour we played an international friendly against Scotland at Livingston. My grandfather was able to come and watch me play live for the first time. Playing football in the backyard in Sydney with my siblings and friends I could never have imagined that happening. Not in my wildest dreams.

After the international, my grandfather organised for me to watch a game with him. Unfortunately, Hearts were playing away that weekend and so we saw Livingston play Dundee United. The stadium had thousands of screaming fans, such an incredible atmosphere. At half time, Granda had organised there to be a tribute to me which was special. A moment in my life I will cherish, especially now that Granda has passed.

Supporting Hearts meant so much more to me than simply following a team: it set me on the path to my career as a professional footballer.

When I watched those videos as a kid, I too wanted to play on that big stage. In 1996, when I was only 14, I got to play for Marconi Stallions Women's. Marconi were, and still are, a big club in Australian football. They played in the Australian National Soccer League and now in the National Premier League, the level below the 'A' League. The men's team had stars like Craig Foster, Andy Harper and Francis Awaritefe, who were heroes of mine. They, along with the Hearts players I grew up watching on those old VHS tapes, inspired me to work hard and achieve my dream of one day playing for Australia.

When I got the chance in 1999 to debut, as a 16-year-old against China, it was a dream come true, especially wearing the green and gold and singing the national anthem. I went on to play 139 times for Australia. Playing for my country gave me the desire and passion. I had very few female footballers I could look up to because we had such little television coverage of football in Australia.

I was determined to be a role model for young girls and inspire the next generation. Fortunately, the Olympics came to Sydney in 2000. I was privileged to play for Australia in front of packed stadiums alongside legends like Alison Forman, Julie Murray and Cheryl Salisbury. The Olympics football tournament was a great showcase for the game in Australia.

Today we are lucky—games involving the Matildas and the teams in the A-League Women's competition are so accessible to the everyday fan. Players like Lisa De Vanna (now retired), Sam Kerr and Ellie Carpenter are attracting a new generation of fans to the women's game and inspiring youngsters to take up football. They will be heroes to little girls and little boys out there.

My football adventures took me to the USA, Denmark and Sweden for club football. With the Matildas I got to travel all over the world and play the game I love. Sharing some amazing memories with teammates, the uplifting feelings of winning together and the anguish of losing together.

Eventually, in 2008, after my overseas adventures, I got to play in my own domestic league in Australia, the then newly established W-League. I played for and captained Sydney FC and then went on to play for Western Sydney Wanderers. It was exciting for me to know there were little girls and boys watching Sydney FC and the Wanderers play and being inspired, a bit like me when I used to watch Hearts and Marconi when I was a little girl.

The pathway is now clear for any aspiring player wanting to chase, follow and achieve their dreams. They don't need to watch an old VHS tape; they can go to the game or watch live on TV.

I never got the opportunity to play for Hearts. However, I do follow the results of the Hearts Women's team. I was thrilled when they were formed in 2009. Equally so in 2019 when they were promoted to the Scottish Women's Premier League.

My footballing journey was an amazing one and something I am so grateful for. Playing for my country will be forever in my heart but I won't forget where it all started. Glued to the TV in the lounge room with those old VHS tapes from Granda watching Hearts and the top 100 goals from the Scottish Premier League.

Keith Hackett
(Sheffield Wednesday FC and Penistone Church FC)—Retired Referee

Keith Hackett is a retired Premier League and FIFA list referee and is counted among the top 100 whistlers of all time.

His refereeing career began in local Yorkshire leagues in 1960, and he reached the English Football League list in 1972. During his career, he took charge of all the major matches in the English game—Charity Shield (1984), League Cup final (1986) and the FA Cup final (1981). In 1981, he was promoted to the FIFA list to officiate international games at club and country level and enjoyed that status until the compulsory FIFA retiring age ten years later. It's a mystery as to why Keith never reffed at a World Cup, but he covered every other international competition including the Euros (in Germany) and the Olympics (in Korea) in 1988.

I wonder when referees get together for a natter if they talk about *"The best goal I've reffed"*? Many, many football fans reading this book will be saying "Wow!" when they see the photo that accompanies Keith's piece. Yes, he was in charge when Ricky Villa scored what some people would choose as the best FA Cup final goal. This was a replay—the first game had been drawn. Just think, the penalty shoot-out of today would have robbed us of that magic. As Keith is wont to remind us, though, earlier in the game Manchester City took the lead with a sumptuous volley by Steve McKenzie that would grace any game.

After retirement, Keith worked as an assessor before taking on the role of general manager of the Professional Game Match Officials Board (now known under the acronym PGMOL) which handles all matters related to the refereeing of professional football in England. He held this position for six years. He was instrumental in referees becoming professional. This didn't simply mean getting paid! Under Keith's guidance PGMOL moved to operating on an equivalent level to the very best football clubs. The best in training and development programs. Engaging health, dietary and psychological expertise as well as video analysis of performance are just a few key areas. Headset communication between referees and assistants and goal line technology are among the innovations he was closely involved with. Keith has become a leading educator and trainer for referees. He has published books, articles and been interviewed for podcasts. He is well known as the wordsmith (questions and answers) of the popular cartoon series, *You Are The Ref,* in *The Observer* newspaper drawn by artist Paul Trevillion.

In *Football Fans,* Keith shares the honour of the Wembley Cup final appointment and the poignant moment when he refereed at Hillsborough Stadium—the home ground of Sheffield Wednesday, the team he has followed since boyhood. He also reminds us that football is more than the big time with recollections of his local club Penistone Church FC (PCFC), a notable grassroots football club. They play in the Premier Division of the Toolstation Northern Counties East Football League, Level Nine on the national pyramid, and currently Keith is the club president. PCFC hold a distinguished place in the history of Association Football.

From School Field to Wembley

I was at home in Sheffield when I received a phone call from the Football Association Referees Officer, Reg Paine. Reg asked, *"Keith, what are you doing on the 9th of May?"* My answer was to say I don't know but will have a look in my diary. Reg continued, "*I am delighted to inform you that you have been appointed to referee the 100th FA Challenge Cup Final at Wembley Stadium on Saturday, 9th May 1981. Many congratulations.*"

Quite frankly I was gobsmacked and eventually I gathered myself together and responded with, *"I will be delighted to accept such a huge honour and challenge."*

I had started my refereeing career in Sheffield in 1960 with little ambition to reach the top group of English referees. This appointment reflected the 12 years I had spent learning my craft in grassroots football in Sheffield.

Many experts record Sheffield as the home of football. Yes, Sheffield FC (not Wednesday or United) is the oldest football club in the World and Hallam FC play at Sandygate Lane, Sheffield—the oldest football ground in the world.

On my journey to the top, I had officiated both finalists—Manchester City and Tottenham Hotspur—on regular occasions, but now I was going to run out and officiate on the hallowed turf of Wembley.

In the weeks leading up to the game I was inundated with the media asking questions and doing interviews daily. The Referees Association Secretary also gave me a call to inform me that my new kit would be sent through and that I would be expected to wear it. I drove down to London on Friday the 8th with my wife, who rarely attended a football game, and booked into the Whites Hotel on Bayswater Road, a hotel regularly used by the FA whose headquarters on Lancaster Gate was close by.

Along with my two linesmen David Hutchinson and Alan Jones, and fourth official John Penrose, we attended the historic Eve of Final Rally that was organised by LONSAR, the London Society of Association Referees. Referees from across the country annually gathered at a venue in London to celebrate the appointment of match officials to the final. I informed my colleagues that it was my intention to leave by 9 p.m. at the latest to get back to the hotel to have an early night. Following breakfast on the morning of the game I went for a stroll on Bayswater Road and into Regents Park. The weather was sunny and warm, and I was certainly looking forward to taking part in the game. Then back to the hotel to put on the FA blazer, check the kit bag and then into the chauffeur-driven Daimler for the drive to Wembley. Having deposited our bags I was about to walk out onto the field when Reg Paine announced that I had a decision to make. He wanted to know if I wanted to receive the gold medal or a cheque for £35.

It was a no-brainer. The medal is something that even today I can look at with great pride. I had one scheduled interview a couple of hours before kick-off with well-known BBC journalist, Pete Murray. After that concluded, I was walking across the field when a security man said that Prime Minister Margaret Thatcher wanted to say hello. Mrs Thatcher and her husband Dennis exchanged comments and then the PM said that her husband was a qualified rugby union referee. It sparked off a ten-minute relaxed conversation ending with both wishing me and my colleagues good luck.

I had a light lunch and then made my way back to the dressing room. The exchange of team sheets, checking the bag of balls, etc., my pre-match instructions were delivered and then it was the press of the bell for the two teams to congregate in the tunnel. The walk onto the field at Wembley from a dark and cool tunnel was amazing and the noise and colour intense. It was a long walk to the point at which we lined up to be greeted by the dignitaries and then the National Anthem.

The game was full of tension and ended in a 1–1 draw—Manchester City's Tommy Hutchinson scoring then having the misfortune to score in his own goal. I climbed the famous Wembley steps to be introduced to the Queen Mother, the main guest at the game. This was the first final at Wembley where a draw after extra time would result in a replay at Wembley rather than an alternate venue. My only thoughts were that if I was handed the medal, I would not be officiating the replay. I bowed my head and shook the hand of royalty, and when I did not receive my medal, I turned and smiled. It was after I had returned to the field that Reg Paine said, *"Congratulations, Keith, you will officiate the final replay on Thursday evening."* A few days later, I arrived back at Whites Hotel on the Thursday afternoon and, after checking in, had a light lunch, a walk and then waited for the cars to arrive to take us to Wembley Stadium for the replay.

Night games under floodlights create a very special atmosphere, and the two teams delivered a wonderful match, played at pace and with a commitment and will to win. I intervened early with a yellow card to city's Gerry Gow who decided that he would attempt to stop Spurs Ossie Ardiles.

I was not having any of that, so needed to take a firm grip until the passion and commitment reached an acceptable level. That early card helped to keep the kettle bubbling but not boiling and out of control. This was my way of controlling and managing players and the game. Talking, encouraging, making my presence felt by the players and taking risks with a willingness to apply advantage where and when appropriate. Players accepted the advantages that I applied and the players to their great credit focused on playing within the laws of the game.

The game will be remembered for one of the most iconic goals at Wembley and in the historic FA Cup. With the score at two each, Tottenham Hotspur's Ricky Villa gained possession of the ball and dribbled around several opponents to score. Up to that I had never experienced noise and atmosphere quite like it in a football stadium. I knew immediately that this was a piece of magic created by Villa. It was the winning goal in a match that was competitive and played to a very high standard. Minutes later I blew the final whistle and gathered with my two colleagues ready to take that famous walk to receive our medals.

What was amazing was in that first game I remember where a dejected Ricky Villa was substituted not having performed and, whilst the game continued, I watched his bowed head and clear dejection walking around the perimeter towards the dressing room which was situated at one end of the ground behind the goal. On the Thursday there was the same player going on a mazy, celebratory run after scoring that winning goal.

Yes, I received my medal and treasure the memory of my involvement in these two games.

Sheffield Wednesday

I was born on the north Side of Sheffield and in my early school days was taken by my dad to Hillsborough to watch the Owls. It was a three-mile walk from home to the ground with a stop at the pub on the way where my dad could have his pre-match pint of beer or two and I would have a bottle of pop and a bag of crisps. When I got to Hillsborough, I was raised and aquaplaned over the heads of spectators to the front.

In 1979, a surprise phone call came from the FA advising me that I had been appointed to Liverpool v Arsenal in the FA Cup. At the top-level referees are never appointed to games in their home region to ensure impartiality. Today FA Cup semi-finals take place at Wembley, but in those days, they were at a neutral venue—Villa Park in Birmingham and Hillsborough in Sheffield being the two stadiums often chosen. A semi at Hillsborough was my only chance to take the field there. Frankly, I was over the moon knowing that I would be officiating a game on the other side of the fence. Yes, refereeing in a ground where I had watched many games and even dreamed of playing for Sheffield Wednesday.

Sadly, by the time my semi-final at Hillsborough chance came my dad had passed, so instead of taking the car to the ground (where there would have been a dedicated parking space) I drove to where the home used to be. The area has now been razed to the ground to make way for a ski park (with a synthetic ski slope). I parked the car, got out my kit bag and, wearing the FA blazer, official shirt and tie, walked to the ground taking the same route that my dad and I took in my school days. I didn't stop at the pub but had to answer the odd enquiry from fans who thought I was crazy walking to the ground. I had a tear in my eye when I ran down the tunnel onto the field. It was a no score draw but remains one of my fondest memories.

Penistone Church Football Club

I was less than five years into my refereeing career when I was appointed to a game at Penistone Church. Penistone is a village 15 miles north of Sheffield where I lived, and I didn't own a car, so I elected to travel by train. The trains to Penistone on Saturday, the day of the match, were infrequent and the one I selected arrived at 10 a.m., well in advance of the scheduled 3 p.m. kick-off.

Any other train would arrive after the kick-off time. I walked from the railway station to the ground and met Arthur Lee, the secretary of the club, who was pushing a line marker, ensuring that the pitch was well marked out. *"You're early, lad. Do you want a cup of tea?"* he shouted from the far end of the pitch.

That day I officiated two games; the referee for the 12-noon kick-off had cried off at late notice. Arthur asked me to officiate the additional game and I was only too happy to oblige. The following week I was asked to visit the County Football Association and Secretary Ernest Kangley informed me that he had received a very complimentary letter from the secretary of Penistone Church. It was a real boost to my career and, some weeks later, I received an invitation from Penistone Church to referee the Purdie Cup final. This is the culmination of a tournament involving local clubs played in recognition of a player who sadly had died young with kidney disease. When my active career ended, I started to watch my grandchildren play for Penistone Church, a club formed in 1906 which operates 22 teams of various ages. I was a regular visitor, and I was honoured to accept the invitation to be president of a club that has been at the centre of the community.

Chris Nikou (South Melbourne and Liverpool FC)—Football Australia Chairman (2018-)

Chris Nikou adds yet another facet to what it means to be a football fan. At the basic, as it were, raw level he is like so many of us. Played the game at a young age and became enchanted with it. Captivated by favourite players and wanted to be like them. Probably harboured hopes of playing at a high level but like many of us, again, quickly realised that was not to be. However, Chris has gone on to be involved in football at a different high level—in football administration. In his day-to-day life he is a partner in a leading global legal firm, K & L Gates, where he specialises in mergers and acquisitions, corporate law, franchising and sports law.

He was appointed as a director of the then Football Federation of Victoria (now Football Victoria), serving for five years from 2003 to 2008. He was company secretary of 'A' League club Melbourne Victory from 2011 to 2014 (having been involved with Victory since its inception). He was appointed to the board of the Football Federation of Australia (now called Football Australia, FA) in 2014 and was elected chairman in 2018.

Notable among his activities with Football Australia was being a member of the organising committee for the 2015 Asian Cup hosted in Australia. He was a member of the Review Working Group set up at the request of FIFA to examine and resolve issues related to governance reforms in the national body. In 2019 he was elected to the executive committee of the Asian Football Confederation (AFC)—only the second Australian to hold such a position. He is currently the deputy chair of the AFC Legal and ASEAN Legal committees respectively, as well as chair of the FA Referees Committee. He is a former chair of the FA Women's Committee. A key achievement of Football Australia in recent times has been to secure the hosting rights (jointly with New Zealand) for the 2023 Women's World Cup.

Outside of football, Chris was involved in the establishment of the Melbourne Renegades Cricket Club, one of the teams in Australia's Twenty20 Big Bash League. He served as a director from 2011 to 2018.

When I approached Chris to contribute to *Football Fans,* he admitted to being a Liverpool fan. *"I also follow Sampdoria in Serie A,"* he offered. The latter allegiance being due to following Liverpool legend Graeme Souness when he moved to the Italian side. *"But Chris,"* I gently suggested, knowing his Greek heritage and being a Victorian. *"Wouldn't you like to do a piece on South Melbourne? I would like you to do that if you are willing. I want this book to be the full football story—not just the very top-level teams."* If I'm honest, I might have said, "South Melbourne Hellas," but I won't tell anyone if you don't.

Friends for Life

Little did I know walking into Middle Park in the late 1970s to watch South Melbourne Hellas that I was about to fall in love with a sport that would become central to my life.

For over five decades, soccer—as we used to call it—has become a passion but, more importantly, created lifelong friends, connections and memories. It has given me a close circle of friends who have been with me on my whole life's journey from a very young age. From the first friend I made at primary school—Nick Deligiannis, to whom I would be best man at his wedding—to Ange Postecoglou, who would be best man at mine, and many more. Others in our close circle of friends include Manny Anezakis, whose late father Leon served with distinction as president of South Melbourne, to Ralph Battista, the money man for Brunswick Juventus in the National Soccer League (NSL).

My parents migrated to Australia in 1956 along with my eldest sister—coming in via Fremantle and eventually to Bonegilla migration camp.

As was customary for European migrants at that time, they were willing to work hard to create a future for their families. My parents worked factory jobs from General Motors to Camp Pie (not a real delicacy) until they purchased a fish and chip shop in suburban Malvern in Melbourne. Four other children followed, another sister and three brothers with me the youngest. Life living behind a shop was busy, to say the least. There was little space to play so I jumped at the opportunity to join South Melbourne as a junior player in the Under-11 squad. Nick's father Arthur would come by and pick me up to take me to training and matches as my parents were too busy to leave the shop.

As was customary for migrants, everyone chipped in to help each other settle into their new country of Australia. One of my first memories as a junior at South Melbourne was playing on the fields outside Middle Park. There used to be an army barracks adjacent to the fields at Middle Park. I recall one day we started playing early in the morning and only stopped late in the evening when it was too dark to see. I struggled to walk the next day but gee, I enjoyed it.

Match Day at South Melbourne was always a special occasion. You couldn't tell now, but just where the pits are for the Formula One Grand Prix track near Albert Park Lake stood Middle Park Football Stadium. Home to South Melbourne Hellas and Melbourne Hakoah. Cars would be packed in like sardines in front of the ground which always led to gridlock when trying to leave after a game! Walking into the ground you would immediately be hit with the aroma of souvlaki on an open fire, the traditional Greek way. The first dilemma was whether to buy one from the stall at the entrance or wait until you got to the other side of the ground. There was always a debate as to which vendor sold the better souvlaki.

A seat in the grandstand was to be treasured as the ground was always packed. No matter where you were in the ground you could always hear the bugle from 'Lefteri' which was a call to arms, and then the whole South Melbourne faithful would start the singing and chanting. Some of the lyrics can't be printed here.

South was always blessed with great players, from Ulysses Kokkinos, whose exploits off the field matched those on it, to Alun Evans (formerly of Wolverhampton Wanderers and Liverpool), the extremely gifted Oscar Crino, to the lethal partnership of Dougie Brown and Charlie Egan, and many more.

Throughout the ground stood many migrants attracted by the love of the game and a sense of community. While navigating settling into a new country and bringing up their families, there was a unique bond which always existed amongst the European communities and their teams. For the Yugoslavs it was Footscray JUST, for the Croatians Melbourne Croatia, the Italians had Brunswick Juventus, while the Maltese supported Sunshine George Cross. Of course, there was another great team for the Greek community in Heidelberg United Alexander, but in those days, it was known as Fitzroy United and played out of the Brunswick Street Oval. Matches between Alexandros and Hellas brought out the best and worst in Greek rivalry. Bragging rights were all important.

One vivid memory of a derby match between South Melbourne and Heidelberg was at the Olympic Village in the mid-80s. My friend Nick was striker for Heidelberg and Ange was part of the South Melbourne team. When Nick scored for Heidelberg, I was ecstatic for him and celebrated accordingly. The only problem was that I was standing next to Ange's mum and dad, who gave me the dirtiest look you have ever seen …

I also remember a fast blond striker by the name of Gary Cole for Alexandros whom I would get to know during my time at Melbourne Victory and we would become friends. There are many stories like that for me. People I have met along the way. Some of whom I see regularly, others not so much, but in any event when we do get together, we pick up from where we left off. I know many football people have had similar experiences.

My football journey led me down the administration path. That's a polite way of saying I wasn't good enough to play at the elite level. I think the saying is: *"The older I get the better I was!"*

From my time at Football Victoria to Melbourne Victory, Asian Cup 2015 Local Organising Committee, to Football Australia and now as chairman, I have met many wonderful people both here in Australia and overseas. However, throughout the journey a core group of friends has remained. We have shared history which is priceless. No matter where life has taken us football has been the glue that has kept us together. It is not unusual for us to get together for a meal and watch a game. Our childhood friend, Ange Postecoglou, has become one of Australia's greatest coaches, and now manages the great Scottish club Glasgow Celtic, so Celtic matches are now a high priority for obvious reasons (apologies to my Rangers friends!).

It all started with being introduced to the wonderful global game of football as a young boy at the South Melbourne soccer club.

Brendan Schwab
(Aston Villa FC)—Executive Director of the World Players Association

Brendan Schwab is the executive director of the World Players Association (World Players), which represents some 85,000 athletes through more than 100 player and athlete associations across some 20 sports in more than 60 countries. It is an autonomous section of the umbrella body UNI Global Union and is based in Nyon, Switzerland. An Australian lawyer with specific interest in labour law and human rights law, he co-founded the Professional Footballers Australia (PFA) in 1993 and played an active role in the reformation of Australian football over a 20-year period, including the establishment of a new governing body, new professional leagues, engagement with Asia and gender equality. Before joining World Players, he was a vice president and board member of FIFPro—the world footballers union. Part of this role involved chairing the board of FIFPro Asia/Oceania.

Brendan grew up in a family that is quintessentially Australian rules football. As we see in his piece, his father, Alan, was a prominent and highly respected figure in the game. His Uncle Frank (Alan's brother) umpired the league grand final in 1961 before 107,000 spectators. His brother Cameron was the CEO of Richmond FC, Melbourne FC (the oldest professional football club of any code in the world) and Fremantle FC. His cousin Peter (Frank's son) was, first, an elite triple-premiership winning player with Hawthorn and later Hawthorn head coach and head of the competition umpiring panel. The key to Brendan's story though is the informed, open-minded perspective of his father. That there was a bigger football world outside of Australia that was worth paying attention to and learning from.

In *Football Fans,* Brendan recounts how this guided his football journey and provides an intriguing backcloth to Australia's football story. For me, it was thrilling to read of his father, something of a legendary figure in Australian rules football administration, being inspired by an equally legendary football manager Sir Matt Busby.

In November 2022 Brendan was inducted into the Football Australia Hall of Fame. In a moving acceptance of the honour Brendan noted that he did not do so as an individual, but rather very much on behalf of the generations of Australia's footballers who have united through their union—the PFA.

Unprepared: My Accidental Journey with Aston Villa FC

If not for the relentless—many would say ruthless—determination of the Richmond Football Club to dominate Australian rules football on and off the field, many years would have passed before I would have even heard of the Aston Villa Football Club, let alone become a devoted supporter. Accidentally, Aston Villa was chosen for me when I was four.

My father Alan Schwab was the secretary of the mighty Richmond Tigers in the Victorian Football League (VFL). In 1972, the Tigers were in search of revenge as a precursor to greatness. Overwhelming favourites to win their third Premiership in six years, Richmond was instead humiliated by their archrivals

Carlton in front of 112,393 ardent fans at the famous Melbourne Cricket Ground. Carlton outplayed Richmond at its own attacking and aggressive gameplan, kicking a grand final record score to win by five goals. The tension within Tigerland afterwards was palpable; heads rolled, and we felt it too in our family home in outer-suburban Melbourne. I understood in kindergarten that football was serious business. The 1972 VFL grand final became taboo, and even back-to-back Premierships in '73 and '74 never quite took the bitter taste away.

The defeat gave further impetus to Dad's planned end-of-season trip to England and the United States to study the administration of elite football. Melbourne's *Sporting Globe* revealed the *"Round-the-world Richmond quest"*, with Dad having arranged to meet more than 20 *"top professional clubs ... to study all matters on administration, finance, fund-raising, team management, recruiting, training methods and facilities, coaching methods and junior recruiting methods."* Dad was to return with a wealth of knowledge and insights all comprehensively documented, some new football books to be of vital importance, a wall map featuring the professional football clubs of England and Scotland, and some gifts which included, transformatively for me, an Aston Villa shirt.

The Villa shirt was to become my companion for the entirety of my primary school years. Made of tight-fitting stretchy nylon in the '70s body shirt tradition, it miraculously managed to grow with me and became a talking point of my childhood. *"What shirt is that, Bren?"* relatives and friends would ask, and I would proudly respond, *"Aston Villa, the famous English soccer club,"* to blank Australian faces. *"Villa have won the FA Cup more than any other club in England,"* I would add. Before too long, the same friends and relatives would say, *"You wearin' that Villa shirt again, Bren!"*

It wasn't a classic Villa strip. It was an all-claret t-shirt, with a round blue collar and blue trim on its short sleeves. The name Aston Villa did not appear on the shirt, but it did boast a magnificent and elegant blue lion on its heart. I had no idea what colour the shorts or the socks would be, where the club's unusual but somehow compelling name came from, where it was based or who the club's great players were.

My brother Cam and I agreed to put the wall map up in our shared bedroom. He had received a Glasgow Rangers shirt and a Stoke City bucket hat, the style of which Kerry Packer was to immortalise a few years later with the merchandising of World Series Cricket. Cam wasn't happy to be a Stoke City fan. Looking at the wall map, we both couldn't possibly understand how Dad didn't choose Hull City for us, given they were the Tigers. But that map was something else—the logos of all 92 professional clubs in England and 37 in Scotland were represented geographically. The idea of 129 professional clubs was mind-blowing, as the VFL had only 12. And there was Villa, at Villa Park in Birmingham, with its famous logo boldly stating, 'PREPARED'.

Cam didn't take much of an interest, but had he done so he would have learnt that Stoke City were then a much better bet than Villa. Then a First Division Club, Stoke had just broken through with their first major domestic triumph by dramatically winning the Football League Cup at Wembley. The trophy was also the first domestic medal for legendary England goalkeeper Gordon Banks, with the winner scored by the great George Eastham, the very same player who had courageously brought down England's player retain and transfer system[8] with the Professional Footballers Association and who I had the honour to meet in 2015 as part of my work for the player union movement.

The only access we had on TV to English soccer in the '70s was the annual live broadcast of the FA Cup final and a short segment with an English journalist named Freddie Villiers each Sunday on *World of Sport*, a VFL-dominated sports program that valued boxing, wrestling and wood chopping above soccer. The FA Cup final would kick-off at midnight, and Dad would host a party every year. The greats of Australian rules football, including Tiger immortal Royce Hart, would sit transfixed to the small screen. For 90 minutes, soccer in Australia was not, as Johnny Warren famously called out, a game only for *"Sheilas, wogs and poofters"*.

Villa, of course, never made the Cup final in that era and nor did they ever

---

8 The case was *Eastham v Newcastle United Football Club Ltd* [1964] Ch. 413; the decision based on the law related to restraint of trade. Bosman was not the first!

rate a mention by Freddie Villiers. I had to look elsewhere for clues, and they were to be found in Dad's library. Dad collected the *Rothmans Football Yearbooks* from inception, and his visit to Aston Villa came shortly after Villa's triumphant 1971–72 season in which the Villans had become champions of … the *Third Division!* That lowly status did not prevent Villa from celebrating the title at Villa Park with a 1–0 victory over Chesterfield before 45,567 fans. According to the *Rothmans*, *"Villa, gaining staggering support from the fans, came bursting out of the Third Division with an authority that left observers wondering only how they got themselves down there in the first place."*

Dad's journal of his trip reads, *"Aston Villa, in the strong, football-minded City of Birmingham, is typical of a club, which because of sloppy administration was allowed to sink almost to the depths of despair."* Dad met with manager and Villa legend Vic Crowe, whom he found to be "extremely courteous", and Commercial manager Eric Woodward. Incredibly, among the reforms under consideration to financially resurrect the club was the sharing of grounds. Woodward revealed that he had *"talked at great lengths with neighbouring Birmingham City who are interested in the idea."* A 1960 history of Aston Villa in Dad's library perhaps said it all: *"Aston Villa's motto, inscribed beneath the club crest of a rampant lion, traditionally linked with their earlier Scottish associations, is 'Prepared'. Yet, in a history spanning the greater part of a century there have been marked periods when the Villa have been singularly unprepared."*

Not surprisingly, Dad did not model his career in sports administration on Aston Villa. It was Sir Matt Busby's achievements at Manchester United that truly inspired him. Busby built three great teams at United, by recruiting, training and developing players from the youngest of ages, and dominating junior competitions such as the FA Youth Cup. Busby also entered the transfer market when he needed, such as when he recruited Tommy Taylor from Barnsley in 1953 for £29,999 and Denis Law from Torino in 1962 for £115,000 (both then record amounts). *Father of Football*, David Miller's biography of Busby, was Dad's Bible. Busby's recovery from the tragedy of Munich to win the 1968 European Cup a decade later was, in Dad's mind, the greatest achievement in the history of professional sports. Although we only knew them in books, we mourned the 'Busby Babes', and Duncan Edwards in particular.

As a distant Villa fan, I felt shame at how United were denied the double in the 1957 FA Cup final when the Babes were at their peak. Dad had his Busby-like moment when Richmond won the 1973 VFL grand final with their lusted revenge over Carlton and, on the same day, won the Reserves, Under-19s, and Under-17s competitions, the only time a club managed that achievement. He loved the kids who came through the system at Tigerland, but was always happy to ensure he could 'pinch' some stars from the other clubs to join them.

My most reliable source for following the Villa remained the *Rothmans Football Yearbook*, and I could learn about each season the year after it was played. By 1975, we were back in the First Division and then, with 14 players, Villa won the title in 1980–81 for the first time since 1910. Dad had a mate in Birmingham who sent through all the local papers, with colour photographs of Ron Saunders and Dennis Mortimer holding the Football League championship trophy on the balcony of the Birmingham Town Hall. Dad and I got up at 4 a.m. to watch Villa win the 1982 European Cup final live on TV. Gordon Cowans was unquestionably my favourite player, and I had the thrill of watching him play for England against the Socceroos in Melbourne not long afterwards. The Villa strips (home and away) were glorious. Was there a better brand in the '80s than *Le Coq Sportif*? I proudly wore both at my Under-14 training sessions.

Dad tragically passed away in 1993 at the age of 52. He planted the seeds for my love of football and is a big reason why I have dedicated much of my career to the game here in Australia. A bit like resurrecting the Villa, transforming Australia from being a great sporting nation into a great football nation is a noble pursuit because so many people care, and its impact can transcend the game. I would have loved to have gone to Villa Park with Dad. I have now taken my sons Matthew and Henry there, and they too love the Villa. I try to get there at least once a year and managed to get across to England for the 2015 FA Cup final. In my work for the player union movement, I have quietly loved it when some Aussies have played for 'my club'. Mark Bosnich, Chris Herd, Brett Holman and

Mile Jedinak have all shared with me just how big a club Villa is, and how that's not fully understood unless you are there.

But size and support do not automatically correlate with greatness, and Villa fans know this better than anyone. There is a famous story often quoted in business strategy from when US President Kennedy first visited NASA in 1962. During his tour, he met a janitor carrying a broom and casually asked the man what he did for NASA. *"I'm helping put a man on the moon,"* the janitor replied. I still love a good football shirt and like to buy gifts for friends featuring a legendary name and number from the past. Once, I was at the Old Trafford megastore and asked for EDWARDS 6. The young bloke serving me replied, *"Fucking quality!"* A few weeks later I was at Villa Park buying a shirt for my son Ben. I asked for COWANS 10. *"Cowans?"* was the reply. *"How do you spell it?"*

Carol Shanahan OBE
(Port Vale FC)—
Co-owner of Port Vale Football Club

A 'force of nature' is possibly an overworked and overused term. Sometimes, rarely perhaps, it is the only suitable epithet to describe a person.

I looked it up on Google: *"To say a person is a force of nature means the person is a very strong personality or character. In short, a person that is full of energy, unstoppable, and unforgettable."* Yes, that will do for Carol Shanahan.

Carol, and her husband Kevin, through their company Synectics Solutions, are the owners of Port Vale Football Club. Port Vale, located in the town of Burslem in North Staffordshire, are my team, my club—have been for well over 60 years. We have had many owners and, not unlike with many clubs, one is left wondering why people own football clubs. Is it a money-making venture? Is it vainglory? What are the owners' ambitions for the club? In just over three years of ownership, the Shanahans have given a vivid demonstration of what football club ownership means to them.

The tales of dodgy business practice by football club owners have become commonplace. I have pondered on the thought: If you could, what business background of your club's owner would you choose? It strikes me that the field of financial technology and data security is admirable. If, for example, banks and government departments entrust your company with data security—and Synectics Solutions does indeed enjoy such trust—then you do have a reputation to maintain. I would aver that the Vale is in safe hands.

Carol and Kevin's success in business has brought recognition in terms of industry awards. For Carol an honorary doctorate and an adjunct professorship at a local university. Latterly, she was honoured with an Order of the British Empire for her community work. At the United Kingdom's Women of the Year Awards in 2022 she was recognised as the Community Heroine of the Year. She is regularly called up by television and radio to comment on football administration.

Carol is what I call a 'we' rather than an 'I' person. In her piece Carol mentions her ethos that, as the owners of Port Vale, she and Kevin are the custodians of a community asset. Further, how that custodianship brings with it community responsibility.

At the start of the pandemic with football across the United Kingdom closed, she told me that she gathered the club staff together and challenged them. *"We can just go into hibernation and restart when football is back, or we can do something. How do you want to answer people when they ask: 'What did you do during the pandemic?' We closed up? Or we did something?"*

I can tell you that the answer resulted in over 400,000 meals being provided to needy families in the local area. In addition to the provision of cooking facilities, club staff and players called up supporters to check on their well-being. It was 'we'—the community—they did something. Port Vale Football Club was the English Football League's Community Club of the Year for season 2020/2021.

In *Football Fans,* Carol Shanahan takes us on her journey from going through the Albion turnstiles on her own at nine years old to owning Port Vale FC—a football journey.

From West Bromwich to Burslem

My football journey is in many ways unique. It started on the terraces at West Bromwich Albion and ended up with myself and my husband Kevin owning a professional football club—Port Vale FC, an English Football League club based in Burslem, one of the six towns of the Potteries, or Stoke-on-Trent, to give it its proper title. Rather than owning the club, however, I see us as custodians of a community asset which is much more than 11 blokes kicking a bag of wind around on a Saturday afternoon. My journey has shown me that football is so much more than a game.

My parents separated when I was six. I was born in Lincolnshire but moved to West Bromwich with my mum when I was eight. She became secretary for a group of GPs, one of whom was club doctor at the Albion. We lived on the Birmingham Road in West Brom and as a nine-year-old I used to walk down to the ground and pay my money to go into the Brummie Road End behind the goal at The Hawthorns—that's how I began. I was very independent as a nine-year-old, I used to go on the bus on my own to school. If West Brom played away I would get on the bus and go to watch Wolves or Aston Villa, so I was never a true West Brom fan, I was just a football supporter. I'm very big on belonging and I felt that on a football terrace, especially with the home fans behind the goal, that's where you got that real sense of belonging and I loved being part of that. I used to push my way to the front and fans would let me through—sometimes they would lift me up to sit on one of the barriers!

These were the days of Jeff Astle and Bobby Hope when Albion won the FA Cup in 1968. That was my last year at junior school and the whole of West Bromwich was blue and white; it gave a sense of positivity with the whole town doing well. When the team came through the town with the Cup, I followed the bus all the way down to the Town Hall. At that very early, impressionable age I learnt the power of football and I don't think there's anything else in the world that has the power to bring people together in that way.

Then I moved back to Lincolnshire where the local team was Grimsby. It was too far to go but when I went to college in Lincoln, I lodged with a lady who did the laundry for Lincoln City. I used to go to the matches there when Graham Taylor was the manager, and they were on a great run of success. Again, that level of success saw the city on a great high because of the football club. One of my biggest claims to fame is that I was seeing one of the players (this was well before the days of WAGs!) and Graham Taylor told him to stop seeing me because I was a bad influence! I didn't stop, it just added a bit of extra spice to the relationship!

I always stood up on the terraces at games. In the season following the Albion Cup win my mum's boss, Dr Bottomley, took me to my first European game in the Cup Winners' Cup against Dunfermline. We were in the Directors' Box, and I remember thinking, *ooh this isn't so good, sitting down*. To me, football is a standing game where we are now made to sit.

The thing that ruined football for me was the Premier League and the TV takeover of games. I really went off it for a while and stopped watching it. Kevin would go off to matches but my job was just to make the picnic for him and his friends. I'd given up on football to a large extent. Then we moved our IT business to the building next to Port Vale FC and I started to do work in the community. The car park was shared by our company and Vale fans on match days but there were issues with the owner of the club at that time which caused problems. I decided to try to sort this out so spoke to my friend Sue who was an ardent supporter of the club. I wanted her to teach me all about Vale, its history and its place in the community. She took me to a match and before the game she walked me all the way around the ground telling me about the history of the club. We bought tickets for the Paddock and bumped into some of my employees who asked what on earth I was doing there. They told me I couldn't go into the Paddock because that's where the "lads" go. I replied that was exactly where I wanted to be!

We sat near the halfway line and when I saw young Enoch Andoh running down the wing I was hooked again. My legal director, a lady who knew nothing about football, came with us that day and thought the fans of the two teams were being friendly when they waved at each other. I had to point out that this was a two-fingered wave because they hated each other—football is so tribal!

At that time, the club had an owner who did not have the same emotional attachment to Port Vale as the fans. There were demonstrations against his ownership, and we decided to make an offer to buy the club from him. It was rejected and after some toing and froing we walked away. The protests continued but the owner was very disparaging of them and stayed put. I was behind the goal at Cheltenham for one match when I saw two fans who were leading lights in the protest group so I went to sit behind them to offer whatever help I could behind the scenes. They explained that without an alternative ready to take over from the owner, their protests were pointless. Others joined with them, pleading with us to do something to help. They were so passionate about the club that, as Kevin and I drove home up the M5, we agreed that we had to try again for those fans. That was our epiphany. We knew that the fans would be behind us, and we wouldn't be in it on our own. Those fans have continued to be hugely supportive and during the pandemic bought over 4,000 season tickets, leaving their money in the club despite not seeing a single game during the season.

The owner then went on a long rant on local radio announcing that the protestors would have their way, he would be gone at the end of the 2018–19 season and would liquidate the club if no new owner could be found. We finally managed to get him to agree to a deal, hugely overpriced though it was, and against the advice of our solicitors, financial advisors and accountants. All of them told me it was a terrible deal, it was too risky, *it could all go wrong, he's giving you nothing.* I told them I'd taken all their advice on board, but we simply had to pay the ransom.

I have absolutely no regrets about what we have done. The day the takeover was finalised saw a huge outburst of support from our fans everywhere—the previous owner would never have experienced the joy I felt then and the support we got from all those fans who had been desperate for change at the club. It was a day of celebration.

During our first season in charge of the club we drew Manchester City, the

Premier League Champions, in the third round of the FA Cup at the wonderful Etihad Stadium. When our centre forward Tom Pope scored a brilliant headed goal to equalise for the Vale, 8,000 fans just erupted in the away section. I was in the Directors' Box, and I just looked towards them thinking, *I want to be there.* Many people, like the previous owner, think football is about money, but it isn't. It's about the people. Prior to the game, Kevin and I had gone to Vale Park and called in on almost all the buses which were leaving for the game because we knew that was the only interaction, we would get with the fans that day and it was so important to us.

The season when COVID damaged football so badly was hard to bear, but the support we had throughout was amazing. I have been asked if it's a season I want to forget but it isn't. I regard the season as our turning point. The period between November and February when results were appalling was the hardest, most painful period of my life. I've given birth four times but that was nothing in comparison to those months! And I couldn't get away from it—I was on a long country walk with my son Patrick after a particularly bad result the night before. There was no one else for miles around until this jogger ran towards us and shouted, *"Trying to forget about last night, Carol?!"*

I spent the whole season sitting in Directors' Boxes in empty stadiums trying to convince myself that it was OK to watch football without fans, but it wasn't. It wasn't at all and never had been. When I was at the first game back with fans allowed into Vale Park, I just burst into tears to see them. Fans are the bedrock of football and without them, the game means nothing.

As I write this, it is just over two years since Kevin, and I bought the club. It is incredible how committed our family has become in that time. As an example of this, we played Cheltenham in the FA Cup in our first season. Although we didn't know it at the time, this was the game that was to lead to the great tie at Manchester City. I managed to fall down the steps heading to my seat at the start of the game. I got rather stuck and had to be heaved out. By half time, with Vale losing 1–0, I was in such pain that I was taken to the Medical Room where I was ministered to by a nurse and doctor. Suddenly we heard a loud cheer and I said, "*You must have scored.*" The nurse replied, *"No, that's you, our lot don't make that much noise."* Then my son, a former fan of Manchester United, who has seen the error of his ways, burst in shouting *"Popey's scored!"*

The doctor told him he shouldn't be there, but Patrick ignored him. Three minutes later the door shot open again to reveal Patrick yelling, *"He's scored again, we're winning!"* Another five minutes passed and there he was again, *"He's scored a third, it's a hat-trick!"* At that point the doctor expressed concern about my raised pulse rate. The man simply didn't understand at all!

I was asked recently what the difference is between owning a club and being a supporter in the stands. I have to say the COVID season was the time when I was transformed from being a fan into becoming the leader of Port Vale. Being a fan hijacks the independent, clear thinking you must keep at all times. This is where many clubs have suffered when results don't go their way. The main thing I've learned in my role as chair of the club is how much supporters don't know or can't know about what goes into our decision-making. Fans often criticise decisions without knowing the background—that is not a criticism of the fans, it's just a fact that so much of what goes on behind the scenes at a club has to stay within the club and can't be shared with supporters. Sometimes when the club is criticised, I want to say, there is another side to this, but I can't, and it can be frustrating at times.

I have spent more than 50 years being involved in football. As my daughter tells me, football is a faith-based system—you pick your team and if you are a proper fan, you follow that team religiously through thick and thin. I talk about 'cradle fans' who come to the club as a child and it stays with them forever. But there are also converts like me who come later and question everything because they want to learn more, but this allows for change and growth, so both are important. I may have taken a while to settle on Port Vale, but now it's in my blood and will be for the rest of my life. I have had some wonderful experiences in football and, as they say in Burslem, *non, je ne regrette rien!*

Journalists and Writers

Tim Gavel OAM (Tottenham Hotspur)—Sports Commentator

The compilation of an introduction to Tim Gavel's piece in *Football Fans* has been among the most difficult of tasks. Where do you start and where do you stop?

Tim Gavel is a 30-year veteran of sports commentating on the ABC (The Australian Broadcasting Corporation, the national broadcaster in Australia). He has covered seven Olympic Games (from Barcelona in 1992 to Rio de Janeiro in 2016) and seven Commonwealth Games (from Victoria in Canada in1992 to Gold Coast in Australia in 2018) as well as the Paralympics at Sydney in 2000. At those games he has commentated on such varied sports as hockey, rugby 7s, sailing and modern pentathlon.

He has commentated on all the football codes—and, yes, on football internationals involving the Matildas and the Socceroos.

His preferred sports as a participant were rugby (union and league) and cricket as a schoolboy and young adult. He now navigates a small white ball around a golf course.

He grew up on a farm near Condobolin in country New South Wales. Hard work, quite simply, was what you did, and Tim would say this has been the backbone of his career in broadcasting. Dubbed 'Tireless Tim' by his ABC colleague Tim Lane—this was a tribute not only to his ability to pick up the ball (pun intended) for any sports commentary at any time, but also to his many involvements with community work.

All he ever wanted was to be a radio announcer and in his early career this included work in radio stations and TV stations across New South Wales and Queensland. From 1988 until 2018 he was 'the voice of sport' in Canberra for the ABC.

He worked at Wimbledon at the 1981 Championships, putting up the nets and the green Slazenger backdrop. If you check your dates, you will see that Tim tested the ball with which John McEnroe ended Bjorn Borg's five-year winning streak! He returned to Australia to work in country radio and television before joining the ABC as a commentator in 1988. He retired from his position with the ABC in 2018 and now works as a media and communications consultant.

Fans of *Cricket on the Radio* in Australia via the ABC must thank Tim for being on commentary duty with Jim Maxwell for the Rio Olympics. Jim suffered a stroke on the air, and, thanks to Tim's prompt action and astute recognition of the situation, medical assistance was quickly summoned.

In the 2008 Australian of the Year awards, he was named Local Hero in the Australian Capital Territory, and in 2014 he was awarded the Medal of the Order of Australia (OAM) for his services to the community and broadcasting.

In *Football Fans,* Tim delves into why he follows Tottenham Hotspur in the English Premier League and his memories of games at White Hart Lane when he was working in London.

Come on You Whites!

Growing up on a farm near Condobolin in country NSW, I had virtually no exposure to English football except that the junior clubs were named after

English teams. For what it's worth, in the Under-9s I played for Everton. Apart from the name, there was little to stir a conscious thought when it came to supporting an English team. That was to change when, as a 19-year-old in 1981, I went to England on a working holiday.

One of my jobs was working for Slazenger putting up the green backdrop at Wimbledon and other grass court tournaments. In fact, in the lead-up to the 1981 Wimbledon tournament, I tested every ball used on the grass at that event. This was done by physically squeezing every ball.

Living in London, it was hard not to become intoxicated with football. It was everywhere and hard to avoid even if you wanted to. Early in 1981, I can't remember the month, but a flatmate took me to White Hart Lane to watch Tottenham Hotspur. I was entranced immediately, from the walk from the train station to the terraces at the Lane. The terraces were a unique experience with the surge and the crushing feel every time Ossie Ardiles or Ricky Villa came towards the opposition goal.

I was intrigued by the non-stop singing of 'When the Spurs Go Marching In' which continued virtually unabated for 90 minutes no matter what was happening on the field. From that moment on, I was hooked and rode every emotion during the 1981 drawn FA Cup final followed five days later by the 3–2 victory against Manchester City in the replay.

Villa's second goal that day at Wembley is etched in my memory as much as any other sporting moment since. (*Ed: See Keith Hackett's piece earlier—complete coincidence that both mention this goal!*)

The Spurs players in that era remain among the greatest in the club's history, players such as Ardiles, Villa, Hoddle, Perryman, and the list goes on. Ardiles and Villa were not the first foreigners to grace the game in England, but you could argue they were among the first to make such a significant impact. They had come to Spurs as a package after impressing Spurs coach Keith Burkinshaw in Argentina's 1978 World Cup win. To this day they hold legendary status at the club. They were inducted into the Spurs' Hall of fame in 2008.

To this day I can recite the Spurs team on that day—it is close to becoming a party trick—but I mention it here as evidence of the impact the club had on me in 1981 and continues to do so. So much so that you start debating with others whether Paul Gascoigne was worth signing for big money in 1988 only to see him emerge as one of Spurs' great players.

I have been to many games over the years at the Lane but am yet to experience the new ultra-modern Tottenham Hotspur Stadium firsthand. That is a treat in store.

The most memorable games are when we play neighbours Arsenal. The atmosphere rises to a near crescendo level; it is beyond comparison to, say, a sporting event in Australia. The crowd singing an interpretation of Barry Manilow's 'I Can't Smile Without You' at away games is unique and hard to eradicate as an ear worm.

It may be seen as unfashionable, but Spurs fans proudly do things that are different. Supporting Tottenham is a bit like that; every club seems to have a rivalry with Spurs. Spurs fans treat it as a badge of honour.

Ned Hall
(Derby County FC)—Radio Producer

Ned Hall is an executive producer with the Australian Broadcasting Corporation (ABC) working with ABC Radio Sport. Prior to joining the ABC in 2006 he was with BBC London.

The start of Ned's football commentary career was something of a baptism of fire. With BBC London, covering Wimbledon vs Huddersfield in the FA Cup, he was doing 'around the grounds' updates. As the whistle sounded after 90 minutes the teams were all square and the message came down the line, *"Ned, you're on—commentate on the extra time!"* Not sure whether Ned's reply was, *"Righto!"* or something more colourful. This led to him travelling the length and breadth of the country often covering three or four games a week involving the London teams.

In Ned's own words he was *"kicking a ball as soon as I could walk".* Eventually getting to play for his village team in England's East Midlands he came under the tutelage of Steve McClaren. The very same Steve McClaren who was to become Alex Ferguson's assistant at Manchester United and later manager of England. Trials with Derby County as a teenager were instructive for Ned in terms of clarifying the dedication needed to make it in the professional game.

Ned's university education took him to northeast England. An honours degree in accountancy served as a guide to giving bean counting the body swerve and, following an internship with Bloomberg Television, he took up postgraduate study in broadcast journalism.

He has worked in various outlets for ABC Sport and has been involved in all aspects of the live broadcast of sport and in editorial leadership of radio and television output. Key achievements include work as an executive producer on the ABC's 'A' League coverage and, outside of football, World Cup cricket (50 overs) and rugby league. The latter including the salary cap scandal involving Melbourne Storm. Football highlights in Ned's media career include travelling to South Africa (2010) and Russia (2018) as part of the ABC team covering the World Cup.

In *Football Fans,* Ned recounts how he came to follow Derby County—the Rams—and makes yet another contribution to answering that fundamental question: What brings us to follow our team? That first time and what keeps you coming back for more no matter how well (or badly) the team is doing?

The Rams

I can't remember how I became a Derby County fan. My dad wasn't a season ticket holder or regular attender of games. BUT ... he had been, during Derby's glory days in the 1970s. Him and his brothers queued for tickets to watch Derby play Benfica in the European Cup (now known as the Champions League) in the early days of the Brian Clough reign.

However, by the 1980s, with Derby having dropped to the second tier and with far less glamour about the club, they had walked away from being regular attenders. Even though my dad wasn't going to matches every weekend I somehow inherited an obsession with football. I nagged my parents about going to watch a game and towards the end of the 1981–82 season I got taken along to see Derby lose 2–0 at home to Norwich City. I think my dad thought that might crush my desire to go to games but my response at full time was, *"Can we get a season ticket?"* My dad says he's still not sure where I found out about season tickets.

So, the following season, we had season tickets. And as I arrived as a permanent fixture at the baseball ground, so did Bobby Davison. A centre forward who joined Derby after he had spent two seasons in the fourth tier of English football with Halifax Town. And over the next two seasons he was the one bright spark in a very ordinary Derby County side. We escaped relegation on the final day of the season on both occasions before eventually capitulating and dropping down to the third tier.

He was a swashbuckling, all-action striker who would happily thrust his head into a mix of boots, fists and knees if it meant turning the ball goalwards. In those formative first couple of years as a Rams fan he was the only reason to go along to a game. He was top scorer for five straight seasons and was loved by all the fans.

A couple of goals stand out when I think about him. One was in a freezing February—an FA Cup match against Sheffield Wednesday. There is no way the match would be played today. On a frozen solid pitch he threw himself in for a diving header to score Derby's goal in a 1–1 draw.

The other was one of his last goals for the Rams in his first spell with us. Another 'goal first/self-preservation second' attempt against Leeds United to help us secure promotion to the top flight at the end of the 1986–87 season. He won a header—contact with a goalkeeper's fist and defender's head being unavoidable—and as the ball nestled in the net, he peeled away to celebrate with the C Stand.

Shortly after that he left Derby for Leeds. I still remember at the end of one school day being told he was going by a teacher who knew how committed a fan I was. It felt like being told you were being dumped by your girlfriend. I was devastated.

He came back to Derby a few years later on loan and I know all Derby fans, who like me grew up with him, never held his spell away from us against him.

He notched eight goals in ten games and was still a hero to all of us. So much so that I ended up naming my son after him. I was turned down on calling him Bobby or Robert (also my best mate's name) but got the name Davison through. So, Davison Hall is walking around because of a fearless and heroic striker who is basically the main reason I stuck fast as a Derby fan through some very miserable times!

Roy Hay
(Ayr United FC)—Academic and Football Historian

Roy Hay has been involved in football almost all his life—as a player, coach, team manager, club official and referee. He hails from Ayrshire and since 1977 has lived in Australia where he has worked as an academic and a journalist. His undergraduate studies were at the University of Glasgow, and he completed postgraduate work at Balliol College, Oxford. He taught at universities in the United Kingdom before joining the Faculty of Arts and Education at Deakin University in Victoria. In his academic life he turned his field of economic and social history towards a study of sport in general and the football codes. He has published several books and academic papers. Of the latter, I would note one published in 2007. While I was fiddling about working on a personal memoir of how much I enjoyed myself in Germany at the 2006 World Cup, Roy was, very elegantly, co-producing a paper in a peer-reviewed journal (*Soccer and Society)* comparing the differing styles of fans of the countries represented at the tournament.

Roy co-authored with Ian Syson *The Story of Football in Victoria* (2009), and with Bill Murray edited *The World Game Down Under* (2006). In 2014 Roy and Bill published *A History of Football in Australia: A Game of Two Halves*, the standard history of the game in Australia.

Now retired, he holds an Honorary Fellowship from Deakin and continues to research and write about the importance of the social and cultural history of the football codes. His paper on why Association Football has not become the main code of football in Australia has been downloaded by general readers and researchers over 13,000 times. In the last couple of years, he has published two books on Indigenous involvement in Australian football and cricket in the second half of the 19th century.

In *Football Fans,* Roy describes why his heart lies with Ayr United and always will and explains why their nickname is The Honest Men.

The Honest Men

I always thought I was born within a long drop-kick from Robert Burns' cottage in Alloway on the outskirts of the town of Ayr, but it was a little further than that. Memory is the most inventive faculty, as Freddie Jevons, my vice chancellor at Deakin University, once told me.

My grandfather played for Ayr years before it merged with Ayr Parkhouse to form Ayr United. Later he was to have a stellar career with Celtic, Newcastle United and Scotland, captaining all of them. During the First World War he rejoined Ayr, and, in 1925, became secretary/manager of the club. He accused a director of the club of trying to bribe a referee, but when it came to the tribunal, he was told he had no evidence and to apologise, which he refused to do and was suspended *sine die*. The director was also treasurer of the Scottish Football Association but was voted off the executive the following year, something that had never happened before. My grandfather had his suspension lifted but, apart from scouting for Newcastle United, he had no further involvement in the game.

My father was a promising player winning a Scottish Schools Cup medal in his time at Ayr Academy, but that happened just before the suspension of his father, so he was sent to Aberdeen University and took no part in the professional game. As a result of this heritage, I've always believed I was involved with football and Ayr United before I was born, and the bond remains. I have supported provincial losers all my life, including the Geelong Australian Rules Football Club. Its success in the first decade of this century was what I found hard to take.

From the age of seven until I left to join the Royal Air Force at 18, I lived in Straiton, a little rural village about 14 miles from Ayr. At primary school we never had enough players to form a football team. There were five boys in my class—myself, Michael Heaney, John McWee, Peter McMillan and Ian McWhirter—enough for a forward line, but no defence. Even at secondary school in Maybole we struggled to field a football team and organised matches were infrequent, though every break in the school day was filled by games under playground football rules.

The village never had a regular football team in the time I lived in Straiton, but in summer evenings a few younger lads would start playing 'three-and-in' around the goal nearest to the Ayr Road. You played as individuals and when you scored three times, you had to take your turn in goals. Older players would drift along after work and tea and by eight or nine o'clock there would be full-scale matches, upwards of a dozen a side, with ages ranging from ten to 40. On one occasion there was a somewhat more organised game which brought the then Ayr United centre-forward Peter Price to Straiton to show his skills. I suspect Duncan Watson, who was a player of some class himself, had something to do with this event. His father John, and later Duncan and brother Bill, used to drive the general store minibus to Ayr United for home games taking as many folks as could be crammed into the vehicle. Peter Price later had a brief spell in Australia, scoring a hat-trick in his first game.

One game at Ayr that I attended with my good friend Willie McCulloch sticks in the memory. It was a home game at Somerset Park against Rangers who regularly ran up a barrowload of goals against Ayr. This time things began badly, with full back 'Sadie' Thomson carried off with a broken leg early in the first half. The ten men defended desperately for the rest of the game. A long ball was cleared out of defence and pursued by winger Willie Japp. Japp was fast but notably lacking in close control. He outpaced the Rangers defence and struck the loose ball with his knee or shin. It ran along the ground and, when Rangers' keeper George Niven knelt to collect it, the ball struck a divot and rose over his shoulder into the unguarded goal. One of the newspapers the next day had the trajectory of the ball marked by dotted line as it bamboozled the keeper. Somehow Ayr's defence held firm for the rest of the day, for the shock result of the season.

Ayr did have a consistent spell of relative success under the charismatic leadership of Alastair McLeod, who kept the club in the top division in Scotland for the best part of a decade. But Ayr has never won the First Division or the Scottish Cup or League Cup. Over the years the best players have always been sold to higher-level clubs and the transfer fees have helped sustain Ayr's existence. Jimmy Smith's 66 goals in a league season remains the highest individual total in British senior soccer.

The family connection helped my son, Ross, to have a spell at Ayr United as he was recovering from an operation on his ankle ligaments in the 1990s. George Burley and his physio got him to the point of a couple of appearances in reserve matches, but the manager suggested he needed a year with a local junior club to get him back to full fitness and to come to terms with the game in Scotland. However, caught outside wearing only a towel when it was snowing as he answered the door of his flat in Ayr in November, he decided that the attractions of his girlfriend and Australia outweighed his prospects at Somerset Park.

So, it is not success that welds me to this club. Not even the hope. But just a kind of fatalism born of long family connection and a cussedness exhibited by my grandfather that I recognise in myself.

Robert Burns' best-known poem (after 'Auld Lang Syne') is probably the long verse epic 'Tam o' Shanter' where these lines appear:

Auld Ayr wham ne'er a toon surpasses.

For honest men and bonnie lasses.

Simon Hill
(Manchester City)—Football Journalist

In Simon Hill's autobiography (*Just a Gob on A Stick*, published by New Holland in 2017) he admits to 'doing just enough' at school and university. When he took his first job in the media with Red Dragon radio in South Wales, it was as if a switch had been flicked. He was not now just a journalist; he was a *football* journalist. He has since forged a career in radio and television where 'doing just enough' is the antithesis of his approach to the work. There is no-one more meticulous in preparation. His on-air delivery reflects an infectious, vibrant enthusiasm for his chosen craft. He has held positions with the BBC in local radio stations and for its flagship World Service and 5 Live channels. This is where he honed his skills as a football match-day commentator, reporter and interviewer. His last job in the UK was with the ill-fated ITV Sport digital channel.

Simon joined SBS in 2003 as their lead football match-day commentator. After several years with Fox Sports (2006 to 2020), he is now with the new TV rights holder to Australia's 'A' League, Channel 10. The UK's loss was Australia's gain.

He has covered four Asian Cups (2007, 2011, Australia's win in 2015 and

2019), an Olympic Games (2004), and five World Cups (1998, 2006, 2010, 2014 and 2018).

He is widely regarded as 'The Voice of Football' in Australia. He has commentated on some of the singularly important matches in Australia's football history. The win over Uruguay in 2005 that took the Socceroos to their first World Cup finals in 32 years; the remarkable comeback win against Japan in Kaiserslautern in the ensuing 2006 tournament; the draw against Croatia in Stuttgart to take Australia through to the Round of 16 for the first time.

He was born and grew up in the north of England in Manchester. I recall him noting his heartfelt thrill when his first piece appeared in the columns of that great newspaper *The Guardian* (initially founded as *The Manchester Guardian*).

Simon was very generous in launching my first book (*The Time of My Football Life*, by Fair Play Publishing in 2019). His spare-time passion is playing the drums in a heavy metal rock band.

In *Football Fans* Simon describes his lifelong passion for the blue side of Manchester. Younger football fans will only know one Manchester City. Simon knows several—some years of thick and plenty of thin. Try the Racecourse Ground Wrexham on a freezing Boxing Day in 1998 in England's Division Two (now League One), for example. City won 1–0 in front of 9,048, by the way. Simon's piece is a classic answer to the question: Why <u>do</u> you follow that team?

August 17, 1974

I can pinpoint the exact date I fell in love with Manchester City—and football.

It wasn't the first time I'd attended a game. It wasn't a Cup final, a local derby or any game of special significance. I was six years old, and my dad had already introduced me to his favourite team the season before. In April of that same year, he had taken me to Maine Road to watch City against Ipswich Town. I only learned the opposition, and the score (we lost 3–1), many years later, thanks to online records. My only recollection of that match is asking my dad if—after half time—they started again at 0–0, and of playing with my toy cars on the hard wooden seats of the old Platt Lane End. I was largely oblivious to what was going on.

But a few months make a huge difference to a child's mind—and when my dad asked if I wanted to go again on the opening day of the following season to watch the game against West Ham United, I remember being keen. This time, it was different. I was much more aware of the crowd, the occasion and even some of the players. Partly, this was to do with the fact that City had started a revolutionary (for the time) scheme to attract kids called the 'Junior Blues'. My dad had enrolled me as a member during that off-season (number 596—I was one of the earliest to sign up), and in return, the club had posted out bits of memorabilia, including autograph books, badges and photo cards of some of the top players of the day. Of Rodney Marsh, Dennis Tueart, Asa Hartford and goalie Keith MacRae with his shock of red hair.

This had clearly had an impact. Before the game, I had pestered my dad to venture into the souvenir shop, which in those days was a small kiosk-type affair just outside the North Stand. My dad bought me a sky-blue rosette with the City badge in the middle. It's hard now—as an adult—to explain how much of an impact that rosette and that day had on me. Kids are very susceptible to colours, and when City ran out in their sky-blue jerseys, I felt a connection immediately.

In truth, I probably didn't have much choice in the matter. My dad had been (and continues to be at 87), a City fan, man and boy. His father (my grandad) was also a Blue throughout his life—although, in common with many of his generation, less tribal than we became, perhaps due to their wartime experiences; he had also on occasion watched United on alternate weekends. But that had all stopped when trouble started brewing in the late 1960s between the two clubs. Perhaps he felt he had to make a choice—and he was always much more of a Blue than a Red.

My great-grandad, Fred Taylor, had played for City in the 1890s—although whether he played in the first team, or even as a full-timer, I have never been able to ascertain. There is no record of him in any of the City archives, nor of the club's forerunners in those early days, West Gorton (St Mark's), Gorton AFC or

Ardwick. Taylor was an engineer on the old Lancashire and Cheshire Railways and worked as a bookie's runner. My dad only has vague memories of him and his mop of bright-red, curly hair. He died in 1947—but I distinctly remember as a child, my nanna showing me a photo of him in his City kit from around the turn of the century, replete with the obligatory handlebar moustache, baggy shorts and hobnail boots. She passed away in the late 80s, and what happened to the photo I have no idea. But by 1974, my allegiances were set: the oft-quoted maxim of *"Get to them while they are young"* was certainly true in my case, and already my first football hero was ingrained.

Colin Bell was City's best player—and one of England's too. I marvelled at his effortless ability to cover every blade of grass on the pitch, seemingly without ever tiring. I had a huge cardboard poster of him on my wall—his arms folded confidently in the classic City shirt of the '70s. I wanted that jersey. I wanted to wear it in homage to Bell and the others. In those days, fans didn't wear replica shirts—they weren't so readily available. Instead, you had to get what they called the 'box set' of the full kit via the makers, Umbro. I pestered my parents for weeks, and ultimately it arrived—the plain sky-blue jersey, white shorts and sky-blue socks with maroon and white hoops at the top. The shirt didn't come complete with the badge, and so I got my mum to sew one on. I might even have asked her to put the number eight on the back so I could pretend to be Bell, but I don't think she had the patience for that! I must've worn that kit every day for months—and when it got to winter, I had a City tracksuit too. Sky blue of course, with the words 'Manchester City' written vertically in pinstripes from top to bottom in headache-inducing maroon.

That these things stay with me, even close to 50 years later, shows just how important forging that connection between a football club and a child is. The sights and sounds of the Maine Road of my childhood live with me until this day. The City chippy, where we got our pre-game sustenance (chips and gravy, the standard Mancunian fare). The match program, of which I had thousands until my parents embarked upon a long-overdue clear-out some years ago. Fellow fans who sat in the Platt Lane End next to us for years. I didn't know where they lived, what they did for work—but I knew their names, and every week we chatted, and shared the same communal experience. Super-fan, Helen Turner, who sat behind the goal in the North Stand, ringing her famous bell every time City ventured up-field or won a corner.

Post-game, part of the weekly ritual for the football-mad kid was to head to the newsagents at 6 p.m. to buy the *Pink Final.* These hastily produced newspapers (printed on pink paper—perhaps it was cheaper, or just more distinctive?) were, in the pre-internet age, our window into what was going on in the football world. Arriving at the shops just over an hour after the games around the country had finished, the Pinks would fly off the shelves, and I would pore over the pages containing all the day's results, league tables, match reports and feature articles. By 8 p.m., my fingers were often black from the (still wet) ink on the pages.

By the time I was a teenager, I had 'graduated' from the Platt Lane End to the Kippax. The huge terrace that ran the entire length of one side of the pitch, and which housed City's most raucous supporters. For much of the '80s and '90s, I could be found there on a Saturday afternoon—and, on alternate weekends, travelling on the Supporters Club coaches or 'Football Special' trains to away grounds up and down the country. Travelling away was special. There was a real sense of tribalism, representing your club and city on someone else's turf. Of course, sometimes things went in a direction they shouldn't have, and there was trouble. But mainly, it was bravado, beer and banter. I loved those trips.

By the late '90s, things had changed. The Taylor Report had outlawed the terraces. The Kippax was an all-seater stand, the Platt Lane End refurbished and updated with tip-up seats to replace the old wooden benches. I was also no longer able to attend all the games, due to my involvement in broadcasting. On occasion, I would cover games at Maine Road, but I always felt it was an odd experience. I didn't belong in the press box there—my place was in the stands, with my dad or my friends, cheering on my team.

Maine Road is now long gone, demolished in 2003 as City moved to the Etihad Stadium. It's a wonderfully modern venue with no expense spared.

The souvenir shop is now a City Superstore, and the old City—the classic underdog that former chairman, Francis Lee, once said would win *"Cups for cock-ups"*—has been transformed by Emirati money, and now regularly wins silverware. It's not the same City I grew up supporting, but maybe that's no bad thing. Life evolves, and so does football as a reflection of the society in which it exists. Perhaps today's kids will yearn for Sergio Aguero in middle-age, in the same way I do for Colin Bell?

But they can never take away the memories. Of being with my dad and grandad, of stopping off for egg and chips on the way home at my nanna's on bitterly cold January days. Of that classic sky-blue kit and my much-cherished rosette. Of Colin, the 'King of the Kippax', who sadly passed away in January 2021.

When they knocked down Maine Road, a friend of mine salvaged some of the rubble and sent it to me. So now, I will always have a physical part of Maine Road too—the place where my lifelong love affair began, back on August 17, 1974.

Angela Smith
(Stoke City FC)—Radio Presenter and Former Professional Squash Player

Angela Smith comes from the same part of the world as me—the city of Stoke-on-Trent (familiarly known as the Potteries) in the northern part of the Midlands in England. Our city has two football teams in the English Football League—my team, Port Vale, and Angela's team, Stoke City. We bantered when I invited her to contribute to the book—luckily, she got past the reference to me being a Vale fan.

Angela is a former professional squash player and one of our city's sporting stars. At the height of her playing career across the decade of the 1980s she was among the top-ranked players in the world. She won the World Team Championships with Great Britain in 1979. Earlier that same year she was a semi-finalist in the World Open singles—going out to the eventual winner, the Australian player Heather McKay. McKay is a legendary player in the women's game, unbeaten for some 15 years, and many say she is the best player the game has ever seen. Angela is one of very few players to even take a game off Heather, 10–9 in the opener of their semi-final clash.

Angela has the singular distinction of being the first woman squash player to turn professional. This proved pivotal and transformed the women's game internationally. As said by another great Australian player, and former world champion, Vicki Cardwell: *"I played Angela Smith many times, she was an honest player of the highest quality… without her ladies' squash would be in the dark ages … all lady professional players owe it all to Angela … A true champion …"*

In addition to her reputation as a player, Angela was a highly regarded coach, contributing to elite player development in the Caribbean, China, Spain, Africa, Hong Kong and the USA.

Angela has appeared on the very popular BBC TV quiz show *A Question of Sport* and on *Superstars*. Currently, she is a member of the Sports Team at BBC Radio Stoke. She is the Chair of the Supporter's Council of Stoke City and an ambassador for the Community Trust that was instrumental in Stoke City having a coaching base in Shanghai. She is a member of the European board of SIGA (Sport Integrity Global Alliance) paying particular attention to gender, race, inclusion and diversity. In mid-2022 was appointed to the position of general manager of the Stoke City women's team.

In *Football Fans* Angela explains one of the mysteries of life: Why do people follow Stoke City?!

I jest. City hold a place of honour in football with historical connections back to the earliest times of the game we know today. They are among the oldest clubs in the world. Angela's piece adds to the rich tapestry of what sparks football fans, and she recounts some memorable moments of a life supporting the Potters. Secret fact—the first football match she ever attended was a Port Vale game!

You Can't Change Your Team

I love all sports, and from the time I was a small child I have been hooked on football. There were several reasons why, one being that I lived in a street full of boys, very few girls, and it was obvious that if you didn't play 'footie' the options of having a fun time in the local area were limited, or so it seemed to me.

In addition, my parents loved football. They came from an era when you supported all your local teams, meaning that my dad went to Stoke City and when they were playing away from home, then he went to the other side of the city to watch Port Vale. My mother had much more sense, she rarely crossed over to the dark side to watch the Vale! However, I was 'punished' in my formative years because I attended a Vale game due to a lack of babysitters and whilst I can't even remember it, I never forgave my dad. I could have been completely traumatised by that event!

The rivalry between clubs and fans has gone on in all manner of fashions for many years and I was amazed to receive a mail from David, who is a fan of Port Vale, asking if I would like to contribute to this book. Stoke and Vale fans tend not to acknowledge each other! I am delighted to contribute my thoughts.

My early memories of watching Stoke City were really running up and down the wooden stairs at the old Victoria Ground and weaving in and out of the empty rows of seats near to my parents. I would occasionally watch the game when I was told to sit down. Then, one Friday night in 1961, this eight-year-old was told that she wouldn't be able to run around at the game the next day as Stan was back!

That was when my love affair with football really took hold. I can still remember going to the match on that day. I had never seen so many people in one place and I was holding my parents' hands tightly. The Victoria Ground was packed, more than treble the attendance of the last game, 35,974 people in fact, and as I could no longer play amongst the seats, I watched the game. Stanley Matthews was the man everyone had come to see. He seemed ancient to me at 46, but every time he had the ball the crowd waited expectantly for him to perform his magic. Every week I became more and more interested and excited to watch Stoke City play.

I can remember Stoke getting promoted in the '62/63 season with the oldest team in the Football League. Matthews scored his only goal of the season in the final game vs Luton and that made certain Stoke were promoted. He retired when he was 50 and in those times the coverage of football on TV was nothing like it is today. When a testimonial game was organised for him, the great and the good of world football came to Stoke to honour Matthews: world greats like Puskas, Alfredo Di Stefano, Josef Masopust and Lev Yashin. Again, I can remember the evening vividly as Matthews was carried off shoulder-high by Puskas and Yashin. A magical night made even better for me as my dad somehow managed to get every player's signature. That is still amongst my most treasured possessions.

Matthews was a great player and ahead of his time in terms of his training regime and diet. I was extremely fortunate to know him in later life and would like to think that some of his wisdom rubbed off on me and helped me in my professional career as a squash player.

When attending your first football game, most people become hooked. The sounds, the atmosphere, the crowd, the whole experience—it is like a drug. Normally the club that you first go to see is the one that you support for life, through thick and thin—in most cases thin, especially if you support Port Vale! (I couldn't resist, David.)

So it is with me and Stoke City. I will gloss over all the disasters and try to erase from my mind two FA Cup semi-final defeats where we were really robbed and reminisce about a game that I am convinced was to be more significant to me than just the victory on the day. Saturday March 4, 1972. I will spare you the ups and downs of the previous rounds (and there were many, particularly versus Manchester United and West Ham United.) Stoke City off to Wembley to play Chelsea, the strong favourites, in the League Cup final. Stoke attempting to win their first major trophy.

I had declined all previous offers to attend matches at Wembley. I wanted to see Stoke City there on my first visit! Whilst everyone said I was mad, the day did arrive at last. We hired a coach, the whole of the street went to Wembley and we walked up Wembley Way and saw the famous Twin Towers. In those days crowd segregation was nothing like it is now and we did have some Chelsea fans sitting amongst us. What a day! Terry Conroy put Stoke into the lead early on, only for Peter Osgood to level the scores just before half time. At this point, one of the

Chelsea fans sitting in front of me leapt on his seat and started waving his hands into my face. I'm afraid the one and only time that I have ever reacted at a game occurred then; I pulled myself up to my full height and pushed him off his seat. My mum was furious with me, though my dad just smiled. In the second half, George Eastham scored the winner to end our 109-year wait for a major honour. It is the only one; the closest we have come since is getting to the FA Cup final in 2011 when we were defeated 1–0 by Manchester City.

The celebrations after the game were brilliant: players dancing around, fans waving scarves and the bus journey home was excellent. The next day, the team returned to the Potteries and the cup was to be paraded around the six towns that make up the City of Stoke-on-Trent. We watched the open-top bus drive past our street and then a friend and I decided to walk to the town hall in Stoke to watch the players enter for a civic reception. The power of football was evident that day. Around 150,000 people lined the streets to welcome back the team and outside the town hall I remember thinking how wonderful it must be for those players to have the support of the people of the city. At that time, I had just started to play squash and wanted to be as good as I could be, but I have no doubt that seeing the team I had supported all my life displaying that trophy to the fans was of greater significance to me. I wanted to be noticed and quite fancied being on a winner's pedestal too.

It is strange how the road we take shapes our destiny. I continued to work hard at my squash, thinking back to the words Sir Stanley Matthews had shared with me about diet and fitness. I became a British Champion and began to travel the world to compete in events. That was a big wrench. Remember me saying that you follow a club for life? Not being able to attend some games due to my sporting calendar was so hard. In fact, in certain English events, if I could, I would drive to where Stoke were playing just to see 45 minutes or an hour of the game before I had to leave to go and compete myself. More of a fanatic than a fan at times!

I started the ladies' professional world squash circuit; it was either that or teach full time and I was lucky enough to play for Great Britain and England numerous times winning World Championships. I was voted Sports Personality of Stoke-on-Trent one year and my name sits proudly on the Sporting Hall of Fame alongside other sporting greats such as Sir Stanley Matthews and Gordon Banks, who was the greatest goalkeeper of his time, and many feel the greatest ever. I am prouder to say that Gordon also became a dear friend along with many of those players I stood and watched show off that League Cup 50 years ago. Jimmy Greenhoff was my hero but how lucky are we to have had Matthews and Banks, two of the greatest football and sporting icons in the world, play for Stoke City. More importantly how lucky was I that they both became friends due to the power of sport.

Whilst I await another major trophy for my team along with many other fans, we have seen ten great years in the Premier League, an FA Cup final appearance, and European adventures. But I promise you, everyone will remember that first game and why they support that club which means everything to them.

My squash-playing days are over, and I am delighted to be chair of the Stoke City Supporters Council and an ambassador for the Community Trust. I am also delighted to have facilitated an academy for Stoke City in Shanghai. My role on a match day now is very different; no pushing exuberant young guys off a seat when they taunt me (it was just the once, honestly), no screaming the lads on. I am a summariser for BBC Radio Stoke which requires impartiality and fairness throughout, so I have to contain my enthusiasm.

That is until—IF—we ever play Port Vale again. Then I can't promise anything other than 100% *Come on Stoke!!!*

Peter Wilkins
(Sydney City FC)—Sports Journalist

Peter Wilkins was a sports journalist with the ABC (Australian Broadcasting Corporation, the national broadcaster in Australia) for 37 years before retiring in 2017. As both commentator and program presenter on TV and radio he covered Olympic Games, Paralympics, and Commonwealth Games. He covered the widest range of sports imaginable from archery to tennis.

Of the football codes, he has covered rugby league (hosting the ABC's broadcast of the national competition in Australia and three Kangaroos tours to England), and both men's and women's football. In the 1980s he hosted the ABC coverage of two World Cups. He was behind the 'mike' for one of the Socceroos most memorable games—more of that later.

In 2008 he was recognised with Australia's premier journalism award—The Walkley—for an episode on the ABC's television program *Australian Story*. This focused on the controversy involving the Australian women's rowing eight at the 2004 Athens Olympics. It was based on Peter's book *Don't Rock the Boat,* published in 2008 by ABC Books. In 2012, he joined a select band when he received the Australian Sports Commission's Lifetime Achievement

Award for Services to Sporting Journalism.

For 'the call of his career', Peter chooses Socceroos v Uruguay—the momentous night of November 16, 2005, which saw Australia through to the World Cup finals for the first time in 32 years. No argument from me.

To my mind Peter's commentary style transported the listener, conveying the agony and the ecstasy. I was at the game in 2005 and didn't hear the radio call live. As I drove home down the Hume Highway the next morning the sports segment of each ABC news bulletin used a sound clip of Peter's penalty shoot-out call. The sheer anguish when Mark Viduka failed to convert: *"... and he misses. Oh, he misses ... He doesn't even hit the target ... Viduka ... The Dook ...!"* The cataclysmic despair in Peter's voice. It seems to come from deep in his stomach and you can feel the turmoil. But then the uncontrolled joy of victory. His sidekick Andy Harper, the usual measured expert comments put aside, was delirium unrestrained in the background as John Aloisi buried the winning spot kick. Utterly memorable.

In retirement Peter continues to pursue his passions of golf and skiing. The former on his personally designed layout on his property south of Sydney.

For me, Sydney Hakoah was a name on the English football pools entry coupon in the 1960s in the northern hemisphere summer. For Peter, it was the team that captivated him and sparked a lifelong fascination with football. He shares this story with us in *Football Fans*.

Sydney City

When mercurial Socceroos midfielder Joe Watson ran onto Hampden Park in Glasgow in November 1985, he fulfilled a boyhood dream. To play against his nation of birth. There were 60,000 cheering, jeering Scots baying for Australian blood in this World Cup qualifying eliminator—numbers far in excess of Watson's normal fanfare with his Australian club side Sydney City, based in the iconic beach suburb of Bondi.

Raised in Fife, the home of golf and not far from Glasgow, Watson plied his footballing trade with Nottingham Forest, Dundee and Forfar Athletic before emigrating to Australia in 1973. His destination for 14 productive seasons was Sydney Hakoah FC—a club formed by Sydney's Jewish community in 1939. 'Jinky' Joe mesmerised teammates, opposition and fans in more than 270 games.

Watson's time at Hakoah adjoined that of another Australian footballing legend, Ray Baartz, whose stunning club career realised 211 goals in 236 games between 1966–74. Baartz also graced the Socceroo midfield/attack for many a year. As did Jimmy Mackay, he of the stunning 28-metre drive against South Korea which catapulted Australia to the 1974 World Cup. Mackay too wore the Hakoah colours. The history of the Bondi club represents a potpourri of Australian soccer's gestation, littered with legends and trophies, which left an indelible stamp on the national game. John Watkiss, Agenor Muniz ... a plethora of footballing magicians grace the club's archives.

Yet it was in the early 1980s when the Hakoah club produced its most prolific and enigmatic spell. Twice the name changed, first to Eastern Suburbs Hakoah in 1977 with the formation of the national league, then to Sydney City a year later in '78.

As the national broadcaster's youthful 'soccer' correspondent, I spent many fervent Sundays at the Slickers' home ground, the sparse ES Marks field, which was a stone's throw from the famed Royal Randwick Racecourse. Their exhilarating, winning brand of football, delivered three consecutive (National Soccer League) NSL Premiership titles from 1980. Add that to the silverware from the first season of the NSL (then called the PSL) in 1977, and you have the most successful team of the era, a standard bearer for entertaining, ruthless performances. There were many trophies and near misses.

It's hard to say who was at the heart of that Sydney City culture with all the pedigree in the ranks, but Joe Watson rated highly. Short in stature, Watson danced the turf as a frenetic dribbler of the ball, balanced by his superior passing, and as a great team player, who'd set up his fellow light-blue shirts with relentless efficiency.

Anchoring this team of the decade was another former Scotsman, Eddie Thomson, who arrived from Hearts and Aberdeen via US club San Antonio Thunder to play as no-nonsense central defender in the 1977 Premiership-winning team, before morphing into the coaching ranks in 1980. He played and coached in that winning year. Thomson was the personable entrepreneur who moulded Sydney City's fortunes in that era and would later craft the Socceroos, first as assistant coach, then in over 80 matches including two World Cup qualifying campaigns as head coach. Thomson took over from another club legend at Bondi in former Israeli national team member Gerry Chaldi who carried a bright torch his successor grabbed with alacrity.

The 'enigmatic' sobriquet for Sydney City came from sheer frustration over the dearth of fans which supported this high-octane outfit. In those three trophy-laden years of 1980–81–82, the team averaged 2,500 fans at home. And invariably those figures were exaggerated. One popular sidelight amongst the scribes, me included, was to count the spectators. It was embarrassing. Eddie Thomson had a favourite take on the empty stands saying it was the only place in world football where *"The crowd was introduced to the players before the game, not the other way round."* It generated perennial frustration for the club.

President and prominent businessman Frank Lowy and CEO Andrew Lederer were numbed with disappointment. Here was their team producing the most attractive football and results, only to be shunned. The anomaly was just one part of a schism which plagued the game in Australia at the time, based around club identity and placement in a competitive and unique multi-code landscape. National competition metamorphosis, or the idea of it, was a constant.

Jinky Joe aside, many of the names who titillated my footballing senses in that team still flit across the mental archives. Another Scot, Jimmy Cant, was a robust, hard-charging midfielder. Live-wire Jimmy Patikas, signed as a 15-year-old in 1979, played in three title-winning teams. He also ran out for the Socceroos at Hampden Park. So did Steve 'Rocky' O'Connor. By nickname, by nature, Rocky epitomised the sort of heavyweight enforcer you wanted at the back. David Mitchell, also Scottish-born, was one of Australia's pioneering footballing exports. A frenetic attacker, Mitchell had a successful yet brief stint at the club before incurring Frank Lowy's displeasure by leaving for Rangers, even having to pay his own transfer fee. Murray Barnes encapsulated the complete high-energy professional for 225 games and inspired them as a leader both at club and national level where he played 31 times. Then there was Todd Clarke, the affable ginger-haired goalkeeper who also played for the Socceroos and was heavily involved in the fashion industry outside of goalkeeping. Both Kenny Boden and Frank Farina scored at a ratio of about a goal every two games for the club across their meaningful, separate stints. They loved quality strikers at Sydney City.

Including John Kosmina, a tenacious old-school front man whose presence in an around the box in 150 appearances for the club from 1981 left an indelible stamp. Kossie scored 89 times for Sydney City and 25 for the Socceroos in 60 internationals. The back to goal. The skilled trap. The gymnastic pivoting and elusive turn before the potent strike. Kossie admired the success but still laments the fortunes of Sydney City which ultimately led to their demise in 1987 after just one game of the new season. *"It was never about performing to an audience, it was about playing for each other,"* remembers Kosmina. The Adelaide-born striker who had a spell with Arsenal before his rewarding years at Sydney City believed one of the secrets to the club's 'winning culture' was to mould just one or two players into the 'Slickers' landscape every year, making sure it was the right player with the right personality to 'fit the culture of the club'. The club was run by *"successful people who expected success,"* says Kosmina.

Unprofitable, unheralded by the fans and unsustainable, Frank Lowy and the board of the Hakoah club made the decision to withdraw the club from the NSL in controversial circumstances in early 1987. They were unhappy with the dilemmas and the direction of the national game under the stewardship of Sir Arthur George yet seemed to delay their inevitable call to provide maximum pain.

ABC TV's Head of Sport back in 1985 was former Olympic butterfly gold medalist, the late Kevin Berry. He was a delightful man who, having procured the rights at the 11th hour to broadcast the first leg of Australia's World Cup qualifier with Scotland, asked me if I'd like to go to Glasgow to commentate the match. Holding my hand would be Liverpool's very Aussie star Craig Johnston, who had co-hosted the World Cup from Spain alongside me in 1982 on ABCTV. Two of the first to warmly greet my surprise late call-up when boarding the plane to Scotland were 'Kossie' Kosmina and 'Rocky' O'Connor. The game had a habit of putting its collective arm around supporters.

'Twas a grand experience on that chill Glasgow evening despite the somewhat negative tactics in a 0–2 loss to a Scottish team possessing Kenny Dalglish and Graeme Souness in a line-up coached by Sir Alex Ferguson. The 0–0 drawn return leg meant the Socceroos were out.

As they often did in that era, Sydney City provided a handful of players on that tour and in every national team ... and a cluster of great times reporting their fortunes amid a rollercoaster of club emotions in the 1980s.

And subsequent sadness. At 48 years of age, Joey Watson, who climbed a personal Everest at Hampden Park, died before his time. Less than three years later, in 2003, so did the indefatigable Eddie Thomson, who co-hosted the Mexico World Cup with me on ABCTV in 1986. Then the unassuming Murray Barnes. All gone. But they lit a footballing fire that will never be extinguished as part of a glamour club in Australian sporting history: Sydney City Hakoah. Thanks for the memories and inspiration.

Henry Winter
(England)—Sports Journalist

Henry Winter is recognised and respected as one of the leading sports journalists in the United Kingdom. Currently he is the Chief Football Writer for *The Times* newspaper. Before joining *The Times,* he was a member of the foundation staff at *The Independent* and later worked at the *Daily Telegraph*. He graduated in English at the University of Edinburgh, and it is fair to say that his earlier school life provided an excellent background for his journalistic career. He was educated at Westminster School, one of the leading public schools in the United Kingdom. Westminster, along with Charterhouse, holds a place of honour in the history of football—the game more formally known as 'Association Football'; the round ball game, if you will, and, as many would have it these days, the world game. Westminster and Charterhouse were at the leading edge of the development of the game in the mid-1800s. The Westminster/Charterhouse version of the game characterised the rules developed by the Football Association in the 1860s. We can say that, if not in the blood, Henry was very much brought up on Association Football.

His own book, *50 Years of Hurt,* published in 2016 by Bantam Press, charts the England national team's 50 years of history since 1966. Despite a World Cup victory in '66 when Henry was but three years old, the England trophy cabinet has been bare ever since—and it 'hurts'.

His piece in *Football Fans* draws upon his experience in following and reporting on the England national team. His first game as a rank-and-file supporter was Scotland vs England at Hampden Park in 1984. Since then he has attended over 300 England games in countries across the world. He has been present at and reported on eight World Cup tournaments as well as Euro tournaments, Champions League and European Cup finals, and FA Cup finals. As a rough calc I reckon Henry must have witnessed well over 1000 goals. He attends upwards of 130 games a year.

He is a multiple winner of journalism awards.

Henry's piece in *Football Fans* was written in Madrid between two Champions League quarter finals in the 2021/22 season—Real vs Chelsea on the Tuesday and Atlético vs Man City on the Wednesday.

In other writing work, Henry has ghost written the autobiographies of four of the United Kingdom's leading footballers of the modern era—Kenny Dalglish, John Barnes, Steven Gerrard and Michael Carrick.

In this book I have wanted to show the importance of football in the lives of people. At the same time, many people often say, *"it's only a game"*. Henry travelled to Kyiv for the opening game of the Ukraine Premier League on August 23, 2022. The game was a symbolic act in the midst of the war with Russia. Result—Shakhtar Donetsk: 0, Metalist 1925: 0. As Henry wrote: *"This was not much of a game. But this was so much more than a game."*

England: Euro 2020 Reflections

A cocktail of emotions flooded through me as I left Wembley shortly before midnight on July 11, 2021. I felt pride in the way England reached the final of a competition for the first time since 1966. I felt frustration with England's much-admired manager, Gareth Southgate, for failing to react to Italy's comeback.

I felt anger at the thousands of wired, malevolent gatecrashers who tried to force their way in, nearly 2,000 succeeding, terrorising staff and genuine ticketholders. And I felt growing horror as I checked my phone, scrolled through social media, and saw the racial abuse that England's three failed penalty-takers were now enduring.

I cover games for a living; it's a professional passion, but I remain a fan at heart. I've attended more than a third of the 1,036 games England have played in their history. I watched England games as a fan before becoming a reporter and saw my first match at Hampden Park in 1984 when Gary Lineker made his international debut against Scotland. 1–1, Tony Woodcock equalised. Peter Shilton, Kenny Sansom, Bryan Robson were amongst those gracing the England team. Jock Stein and Bobby Robson, the legendary managers. A treasured souvenir of the occasion, a 'Remember Bannockburn' flag, hangs in my study.

As back then, I just wanted England to win on July 21, 2021. I always acknowledge the opposition's strengths, and Italy had many, but always hope that England will win a trophy one day. I'd interviewed Italy's coach, Roberto Mancini, as a player at Leicester City and manager at Manchester City and knew he would make life difficult for England at Wembley.

There were still plenty of fans around shortly before midnight as the England bus moved almost mournfully out of Wembley, and out on to streets still strewn with debris. Most had behaved magnificently, supporting the team unconditionally, appreciating how much the likes of Kyle Walker, Harry Maguire and Raheem Sterling had given. All three were named in UEFA's Team of the Tournament. Others delivered, too, certainly Harry Kane after a slow start, and Luke Shaw, whose early goal in the final gave England such hope. Mason Mount led the young generation of talent that has brought such excitement around England. Kalvin Phillips and Declan Rice brought a fearlessness to midfield.

And this is the key to the new England team under Southgate, the team that made the semi-final of the 2020 World Cup and the final of the delayed Euros. Southgate knew from bitter experience as a player that there was a fear to playing with England: the media pressure, the decades of anxiety over penalties, the eternal club-versus-country tensions. When Southgate took over in 2016, he immediately tried to remove the edge, and rebuild relations between the players and the fans, who had long become disenchanted with the squad. Too many egos, the fans felt. Too interested in their wages, images and clubs, ran the critique from the supporters. I shared many of these concerns.

So, on the eve of the World Cup, Southgate encouraged all his players to tell their stories of their journeys, the difficulties encountered on the way to the squad, the broken homes, the sacrifices, the poverty, the hunger, the discrimination, the mental health struggles and the setbacks with clubs, leading to loans, spells in the EFL, even non-League. The media listened and relayed these moving stories to the fans and, gradually, and with results improving, the England squad was feted as an emotionally literate, hard-working representation of a more diverse society.

Even on the eve of the Euros, when England fans at the two friendlies in Middlesbrough jeered the players taking the knee and showing support for anti-racism campaigns, there was still some acceptance to be had, but during the Euros, the country fell totally in love with the team. They embodied a new hope, a new era.

England have achieved so much as a powerful social force, and it is little surprise to see such motivated individuals as Sterling and Marcus Rashford leading hugely important campaigns tackling racism and child food poverty respectively. England were heroes off the pitch, and just needed to get that trophy now as they headed into Wembley on July 11, 2021.

In the late afternoon, England's bus came off the North Circular Road and skirted Olympic Way which had been heaving since before lunchtime with ticket-holding fans and tens of thousands of others who turned up for the occasion: the noise, the drink and, in some cases, the cocaine.

I walked up Olympic Way and my shoes kept sticking to the beer-stained tarmac. Punters were lobbing beer into the air followed by bottles and fireworks. It was bedlam, and the police presence was minimal. Many of them had been sent to central London where large crowds were gathering. Outside Wembley, lawlessness reigned. Just before kick-off, a surge overwhelmed stewards on the gates and a couple of thousand forced their way in. They knew that because of COVID restrictions that there would be empty seats. They had no thought for the stewards, Wembley staff and innocent fans who were pushed brusquely, even violently out of the way.

For the real supporters, there was so much to admire on the field. It was great to see England taking the game to such vaunted opponents. It was a mesmerising occasion, full of good and bad. There was some exchange of views between rival fans, and the Italians certainly took exception to English eating habits with the banner *'Stop Putting Pineapple on Pizza'.* But then England fans had more to feast on.

Kane, showing the intelligence of movement that has made him so loved as a team player by fans, found Kieran Trippier, another hugely popular character. Talk to Trippier and he will tell you about how England-mad his family is, and how his father got fined by the local council for erecting a huge flagpole to fly the flag of St George. Trippier crossed for Shaw to score on the half-volley and England believed. Football's coming home.

That famous football anthem rings around Wembley and always annoys followers of every other country. They just don't understand it. They think it is typical English arrogance, thinking we own the game (when we only invented it). *Football's coming home* is about supporting a team even when you know things may go wrong. It's about English irony, too. It's about English humour, not arrogance. Anyway, it's such a good tune that other countries have adopted it. The Germans love singing it, slightly overlooking that the years of hurt are partly because of them.

Could England hold on for 88 minutes? Had they scored too early? England were terrific in the first half, Walker and Shaw raiding, Kane scheming and England dreaming. But Italy were waking, and Marco Verratti was getting more of a hold in midfield. This was a film I'd seen before. England promising but fading. England scoring, but then becoming a bit nervous and cautious in possession. Southgate had to respond, whether with encouragement or a tactical tweak at half time.

Southgate kept faith in his 3–4–3 starting formation as his back-three gave Ciro Immobile no room, but the tide was clearly turning, and Mancini accelerated the process. My eyes turned to the Italian bench. On came Bryan Cristante and Domenica Berardi for Immobile and Nicola Barella. Italy switched from 4–3–3 to 4–2–3–1 with Berardi now occupying England's defenders while Lorenzo Insigne and Federico Chiesa moved dangerously between the lines. Even from the terraces, you could see the switch immediately working and the problems facing England. Southgate's centre-backs had no classic Number 9 to deal with and looked confused. Mancini's changes worked and Leonardo Bonucci soon equalised.

Why didn't Southgate respond? That's what many England fans were thinking. He did remove Trippier for Bukayo Saka and move to 4–3–3, then Jordan Henderson for Rice. England fans began singing for Jack Grealish who eventually arrived in extra time, but the game seemed destined for penalties. As someone who has followed England for so long and was well aware of the simmering racism that lurks on social media, I sadly knew what the reaction would be when England's first two penalties were converted by white players, Kane and Maguire, and then up stepped three black players, who had given so much to team and country during the tournament, Rashford, Jadon Sancho, and Saka. The heart fell as each one missed. I knew what was coming their way: filthy, unadulterated racism. English society still has so many problems to contend with.

I could see the abuse flowing their way like effluence from a broken sewer. Rashford, Sancho and Saka are strong characters—you have to be to reach their heights in such a competitive profession—but will they want to take penalties again? Probably, yes. That's the way they are made. But will they recall the abuse as they make that long, lonely walk from the centre-circle again? Probably, yes.

There was so much to take in as I walked away from Wembley on July 11, 2021, as midnight loomed and the grand arch over the stadium was lit up in Italy's colours. There was pride in how England had played, in how they had united the country, but that anger at Southgate's failure to respond as well as Mancini still lingers. As does the embarrassment over the behaviour of the thugs who stormed Wembley and the scum who abused Rashford, Sancho and Saka. July 11, 2021 was a day that said so much about the good and bad in life, and the ensuing cocktail of contrasting emotions that fans feel.

The Volunteers

Eddie and Jean Jackson

(Port Vale FC, Newcastle United FC and Whitley Bay FC) - Volunteers

Some of the contributors to this book are well-known public figures. Some are not, though, and this latter group takes a richly deserved place in the 'honour roll'. These are people who, yes, are football fans to their very core but they also do volunteer work that helps to keep their club going. The big-time clubs don't need volunteers, at least not nearly so much. However, you don't have to reach too far down to find clubs for whom volunteers are the lifeblood. There are many such people around the world. Some of the contributors in this book represent them.

Eddie and Jean Jackson met at Leicester University. Eddie mentioned that he had a game to go to, and Jean had a car. The attraction was only multiplied when, a short time into the conversation, it became apparent that Jean's understanding of the offside law was significantly superior to Eddie's. The rest, as the saying goes, is history. They are both retired schoolteachers and have been married for 48 years.

Their volunteer work at the Vale includes such mundane tasks of putting

'Reserved' stickers on the seats of season ticket holders. They truly come into their own in helping with the production of the match day program. Jean is a written contributor and has had over 600 pieces appear in the publication. Over many years club owners have sought their supporters' opinions on many matters related to the running of the club. Eddie writes a report for every game that is transmitted via email and a website to supporters worldwide. At the time of writing this profile he had written around 1,000 match reports. His predictions for upcoming games appear in the local newspaper.

Eddie is steeped in following Port Vale, one of two Football League teams in his home city of Stoke-on-Trent in England. Eddie saw his first game at the age of five in 1950 and he and Jean have followed them at home and away since they were married in 1974, very rarely missing a game. In a typical season they cover anything up to 10,000 miles (16,000 kilometres). In years gone by it was there and back in one day for most journeys, a maximum of 400 miles. These days, though, it includes numerous hotel nights. The two games they did miss eclipsed the distance record—10,500 miles to visit me and see Melbourne Victory v Perth. Jean's next program piece for the Vale rejoiced in the availability of 'proper coffee' at AAMI Park. But does it outdo the Staffordshire Oatcakes at Vale Park? They have season tickets for Port Vale and Newcastle United. Typically, they attend a dozen or more Magpies matches as well as those for Port Vale.

In *Football Fans,* Eddie's piece is unashamedly about the Vale and his long history of support. Jean starts with her hometown team, Whitley Bay (a semi-pro club from that hotbed of football in the north east of England—the list of great players from the region is long and illustrious). Whitley Bay has never reached the Football League, but they have played at Wembley in three consecutive seasons in the final of the FA Vase, reserved for teams in the lower levels of non-league football. (Needless to say, Eddie and Jean were there for all three victories.) She then regales us with stories of the regional heavyweight Newcastle United. And then there's Vale—she married into it and has embraced it in fine style.

Up the Vale!

There were doubtless many things I inherited from my parents when I was born in Stoke-on-Trent in 1945, one of which is my love of Port Vale Football Club. Mother's brother, Tom Brennan, was a forward with Vale over 100 years ago and he even scored against Manchester United. My father, Ted, was what was then called a wing-half with Vale in the 1920s. He never rose to first team level but was there at the time of Jimmy Oakes, one of our most distinguished players of that era. Lots of people told me that Dad was a good player, but his greatest achievement was winning the big knock-out competition sponsored by our newspaper, *The Sentinel Cup*, with Kidsgrove Wellington. So, the simple answer to what first made me a Vale fan is *"it is in my blood".*

For the first five years of my life, Vale played at the Old Recreation Ground in Hanley, where we lived, so the fact that Vale were very much my local team was an additional reason for my choice of club. Or did Vale choose me?! In 1950 Vale moved from Hanley to Burslem, often referred to as the Mother Town of the Potteries. It was a newly built stadium, not remotely of the quality of new grounds today. What few seats there were were all on one side of the ground. Expectations of future ground development were high, and it was advertised as the Wembley of the North. This is a hope yet to be achieved despite substantial ground improvements.

My dad took five-year-old me there soon after the stadium opened in 1950. Work was still ongoing and there were piles of builder's sand around the place. Dad said I was more interested in playing in the sand than watching the action—nothing has changed!

I don't recall us attending every home game at the time, as family finances would not permit it. I had the unsophisticated approach of a young lad when attending games. Don't ask me about tactics or the offside trap. If Vale scored or won, I was happy, and if they didn't, I was sad. In my early years of watching Vale there was plenty to please me, as Vale had their *annus mirabilis* in 1953/54 in winning Division Three North and reaching the FA Cup semi-final. In this, they played eventual winners West Bromwich Albion, taking the lead before being cheated out of it because of some odd decisions! After this promotion to what is now the Championship, my recollection of individual players and matches becomes much clearer. Local heroes (and in those days nearly every player was indeed locally born) Tommy Cheadle, Basil Hayward, Albert Leake and Colin Askey stick in the mind even now. Vale was managed by Freddie Steele, who gave Vale the Iron Curtain or 'Steele Curtain' defence. By 1958 Vale were back at the bottom level as founder members of the newly formed Fourth Division. What a season that proved to be! Champions and scorers of a bumper 110 goals.

For all my early years, I'd watched from the Bycars End—a terraced standing area behind one of the goals. When I was very young, my dad was allowed to lift me over the turnstile. I doubt we had to pay very often in those days! In the early '60s I moved to the relative luxury of the Railway Stand seats. It cost the princely sum of eight shillings and sixpence per match, equivalent to forty-two and a half pence in new money. No way could we afford the extra two shillings to enter the rarefied atmosphere of the centre Stand.

In 1965, Sir Stanley Matthews became general manager of the Vale with Scottish international Jackie Mudie as team manager. These were exciting times. Sir Stan was a Pied Piper figure. Huge numbers of young players from everywhere queued up to join Sir Stan at Vale, including a number from Scotland, one of whom was the now locally well-known Mick Cullerton. Despite this enthusiasm, reflected in increased attendances, things did not work out well on the field. In 1968, Vale were expelled from the Football League for making illegal payments to players. I can tell you these payments were very much small fry, of the tea service variety. The local *City Times* newspaper started a campaign called *'I'm Backing Vale'*. Anyone who sent in their name had it printed in the paper and was sent an *'I'm Backing Vale'* badge. I wore this badge with pride and Vale were voted back in. Phew!

It was in 1965 that I finally attended my first-ever away game, an FA Cup tie at Oxford. Apart from our coach driver getting lost and taking us to non-league

Oxford City instead of the Manor Ground home of Oxford United, it went well, Vale drawing then winning the replay. My favourite Vale player at this time was winger/striker John Rowland, possessor of the hardest shot I've ever seen from a Vale player.

Gordon Lee gave Vale a few good years and he, perhaps uncharacteristically, brought in my favourite Vale player of all time, the very skilful midfielder Johnny Green. He used to glide across the pitch rather than walk across it! Interestingly, quite a number of Vale oldies share my opinion of Johnny. When he died in 2010, a lot of Vale fans paid tribute to him on the internet message boards. We collated these and sent them to his widow via the undertaker. Imagine my surprise when I received a phone call from Johnny's widow thanking us for what we had done.

There is, however, no doubt that Vale's best decade in my lifetime was yet to come. John McGrath arrived at Vale in 1979, assisted by the relatively unknown John Rudge. John McGrath was great at beating the drum and getting fans on board. It fell to Rudge to take the club to the best position they had held for 32 years, the dizzy heights of the Championship. The first leg of the Bristol Rovers play-off game to take us there was memorable for the draw Vale achieved but also for us having to be taken home by emergency breakdown services after our car broke down near the ground. We arrived home at 7 a.m. having had no sleep and in time to head off to school for our teaching jobs. The nineties remain my favourite decade in supporting the Vale. Some wonderful FA Cup victories. Some terrific players such as Martin Foyle, Phil Sproson, Tony Naylor, Ian Taylor, Paul Kerr and Robin van der Laan, to name but a few. Three Wembley appearances included one of my favourite days supporting the Vale, May 22, 1993, when Vale won the Autoglass Trophy in front of nearly 25,000 Vale supporters. That was almost matched in joy by the victorious tour of the city next day. Rudge put together a team of fine footballers, selling some and replacing them with bargain buys from lower divisions and non-league.

For a long time, indeed since the 1970s, I have been attending nearly all away games in the company of my wife, herself a football fanatic. Gradually we ticked off the various grounds and reached a situation where we had visited every ground currently in the league. We hardly needed a satnav as we had been all over the country many times. We made use of many hotels around the country. Our mileage has greatly increased over the years as you can add our trips to Newcastle United, home and away.

My most recent years watching Vale have provided a lot of disappointment. Some poor ownership led to relegation to League Two. New enlightened owners in the form of Carol and Kevin Shanahan transformed the feeling around the club. At the time of writing, Vale are embarking on another season full of hope and expectation following last season's memorable Play-Off victory at Wembley—now my favourite-ever Vale day.

I've spent nearly the whole of my life as a Port Vale fan. There have been ups and downs, on and off the field. There was the very big low of my father falling ill at Vale Park in 1970 and dying of a heart attack less than two hours later. But there have been so many highs, too.

I've learnt the geography of our country. Would I have located and visited Accrington, Yeovil and Colchester had I not seen Vale play there? I've shed tears of sorrow on leaving Plymouth Argyle after Vale had lost in 1978, sending Vale down and keeping Argyle up. I've shed tears of joy on seeing Vale win at Exeter to earn a place in the Autoglass Trophy Final and then again on arriving at Wembley for the Final in 1993. My Vale—at Wembley for the first time! A wonderful memory to cherish.

I've made many friends through Vale, some of lifelong duration. Vale have never been considered a huge club and perhaps they never will be. Sometimes I hear people say to fans of the smaller clubs, *"Why don't you support a proper club?"* by which they usually mean our local rivals or Manchester United. Just as well all fans don't follow their advice. Fans of the big clubs are dissatisfied if they don't win a major trophy. They will never experience the joy I have felt in following the Vale through thick and thin. I have held a season ticket every year since 1973. Do I regret anything? Not one single thing.

The Bay, The 'Toon and The Valiants

If anyone were to ask me why I'm a football fan, I would have no idea what to tell them. None of my family ever had any interest in football: my brother was a cyclist, very much a solo sport rather than a team game; my father had no interest in the sport and my mother was so unaware of the game that she had a habit of walking in front of the telly when *Match of the Day* was on!

When I was at primary school there was a lad I quite liked, Chris by name, who used to watch Whitley Bay FC, an amateur team in the Northeast of England. I wangled my way into going to a match with him and was hooked—on the football rather than Chris! Whitley played in the Northern League, one of the strongest leagues outside of the 'proper' Football League at the time. The players were all amateur, playing for love and the odd five-quid note pushed illegally into their boots after a particularly good win. During the 1960s, Whitley Bay FC were a power in the amateur game in the north. The club reached the FA Amateur Cup quarter-final in 1965 and were drawn at home against Hendon, one of the most successful clubs in the country at the time and provider of the bulk of the England Amateur international team. The crowd at Hillheads Park that day was 7,301, a figure that has never been beaten. Whitley lost that game but went one stage better the following year, reaching the semi-final again facing Hendon. It was probably at that game that I understood for the first time just how gut-wrenching football can be for a fan. The game was played at Sunderland's home, Roker Park, and, having dominated the game from start to finish, Whitley lost, largely because of a world-class performance from the Hendon and England keeper, John Swannell. I've never forgiven him. In my later years, I saw Whitley win the FA Vase four times, three of them in succession at Wembley, but Swannell is still on my hate list!

Saturday afternoons at Hillheads Park were a feature of my life in the 1960s. I remember one game I attended in 1966 when I had an ancient transistor radio with me because I also wanted to listen to the Test Match between England and the West Indies at the Oval. I was sitting on the grass underneath the barrier around the pitch while Jon Snow and Ken Higgs were in the process of putting on a record stand of 128 for the tenth wicket. Every time the linesman ran past, he asked me the score!

My favourite player at that time was a bulldozer of a centre forward called Billy Wright, not the Wolves and England player. He scored over 300 goals for the club and was feared throughout the Northeast and beyond. Central defenders would have nightmares about him, waking in a cold sweat after imagining Wright hurtling towards them. He once scored a goal by standing on the edge of the penalty area while the opposition keeper took a goal kick. Wright jumped up and headed it straight back into the net!

I was also keen on Newcastle United. Newcastle was the closest professional team to where we lived in Whitley so naturally, I supported them if only from afar for most of the time. My first match there was in 1961 against Manchester United. My dad, realising I wasn't going to be put off, conned me into going to the 'Town', as the city was known locally, on some pretext or other. We met a work colleague of his at the bus station and, without me realising what was happening, we headed straight up to the Cathedral on the Hill—St James' Park. I stood at the front of the Leazes Terrace, almost within touching distance of the players. Bobby Charlton was in the opposition team, and I witnessed him miss an open goal. It was not until the 1966 World Cup that I was prepared to accept he was anything but useless.

At the end of that season Newcastle were relegated from the First (Top) Division. I suppose I should have realised at that point that I could have made a more sensible choice of team. Spurs won the double that year and gained the support of one of my cousins who was clearly a glory hunter. I just couldn't do it. What connections did I have with Tottenham? How could I swap allegiance to a bunch of cockneys just because they were winners? Even as a ten-year-old, I knew that this was not the behaviour of anyone with a heart. You stuck to your team no matter how rubbish they were; to do anything else was the mark of an apostate worthy of contempt.

When I went to university in Leicester, I met a bloke who was astonished to discover that I understood the offside law and was aware of Don Revie's vanishing centre forward tactic. This was the beginning of a beautiful friendship which morphed into 48 years and counting of marriage. Sadly, he had no affiliation with either Whitley Bay or Newcastle United being a lifelong supporter of Port Vale, a team from the town of Burslem in the city of Stoke-on-Trent. Vale were a lower division club whose one moment of glory had been the 1953–54 season when they won the Third Division North championship and reached the semi-final of the FA Cup, only the second Third Division team to do so in the history of the world! One of our first dates was when he persuaded me that, as I had a car, it would be nice if I took him the 30 miles from Leicester to Notts County to see his beloved Vale. The fact that I agreed to this venture suggests that I was smitten with the guy and prepared to overlook his strange taste in football teams.

Upon our marriage two years later, I had to promise to love, honour and have a Vale season ticket. You are probably beginning to see that my choice of teams left much to be desired! I'm now approaching my 50th year of following Burslem's Finest, but I have never forgotten my true love—not my husband, but Newcastle United. We remained regular attenders at St James' Park and various away grounds watching Newcastle when the Vale fixture list made it possible. Eventually, upon my reaching eligibility for the reduced-price senior tickets at the Magpies, we bought season tickets for Newcastle as well. We did this just after the club had been relegated again. I suspect it would be appropriate if I had 'idiot' tattooed on my forehead!

I have seen many wonderful players wearing the famous black-and-white stripes of Newcastle with Alan Shearer being one of the greatest. My first hero there was Len White, a much-underrated centre forward who was unlucky never to be capped by England. One of my best-ever memories, however, is a goal scored by Peter Beardsley at Tottenham in the early 1990s. We were sitting in the home seats rather than the away section, so I had to keep rather quiet as Newcastle went a goal up and I stood and applauded through gritted teeth as Barmby equalised for Spurs. With the game heading for a draw Beardsley latched on to a quick free kick and ran into the penalty area. Three Spurs defenders converged on him, but he must have had a magic force field protecting him as he left them all chasing shadows before hitting the winner. I was halfway off my seat yelling when my better half yanked me back before the locals could punch my lights out! A fantastic moment.

As a girl, I was born too early to be allowed to play competitive football in this country. No Lionesses in those days. Playing in the back lane behind our terraced house with the local lads was as much as I was able to do. That was where I learnt to kick a ball with confidence and attempt keepy-uppy records. As it turned out, my chances of playing at a proper level, even if such a choice had been available, would have been hampered by the fact that I stopped growing at 13 and only reached a smidgen over five feet tall! I would never have been able to challenge for a ball in the air against some of these Amazons that play women's professional football these days.

For some people football is a passing interest. For others it is what they watch on a Saturday afternoon or participate in on a Sunday morning. For me, it has been the glue that has held a wonderful marriage together and provided endless great memories at football grounds around the country.

Victoria Morton (South Hobart FC)—Administrator/Volunteer

Victoria Morton belongs to the special band of football fans that I wanted to include in this book—the volunteers. There is no question that Vicki's involvement in football as a volunteer goes above and beyond.

Her pathway into football was through her sons taking up the game as junior players at South Hobart Football Club. It is not unusual for parents to be involved while their kids are playing and then move on. Not in Vicki's case—she joined the SHFC board in 2003, was board secretary and then became president in 2010.

Vicki's involvement in football now extends beyond South Hobart. She is deputy chair of the Association of Australian Football Clubs (all players Australia-wide in the National Premier Leagues) and president of the Central Region Football Association in Tasmania (covering junior players in the greater Hobart area). Unsurprisingly, Vicki was named as Football Administrator of the Year in 2018. Last, but by no means least, Vicki is a committee member for Women in Football—a national organisation in Australia that exists to encourage, assist and facilitate the involvement of girls and women in all aspects of football.

She met her partner, Ken, through South Hobart. Ken runs the Morton Soccer School and is head coach at the club. Hard to know where Vicki finds a spare moment but when she does, she manages *The Kit Room*, Hobart's shop for all things football.

South Hobart FC is a powerhouse of football in Tasmania and was founded over 100 years ago. In *Football Fans* Vicki tells of her passion for the club.

Football and Love

There can never be too much love when it comes to football. I came to South Hobart Football Club as many women do, supporting my children. I certainly didn't know it would lead me to a new career, a new husband, and a passionate love of my club and the game.

If you hang around a club long enough, you get asked to help. It started with junior coach and team manager roles, moved to secretary and then my current position of president. I have been honoured to hold this role for 13 years.

Late in 2007 we had a scheduled board meeting to interview a prospective first team coach. I was late, rushed in and found myself sitting next to the candidate in the only spare seat. The president at the time said, *"You better watch yourself sitting there,"* to which I replied, *"I can take care of myself."*

This was my first meeting with Ken Morton. After the meeting a few of the board were apprehensive about offering the job to Ken. *"He is overqualified." "He won't stay." "Why would he want to coach at South Hobart FC when he could go back overseas and continue coaching professionally?"*

We voted, and he was narrowly appointed to the job which, incidentally, paid no wages. It was the best modern-day appointment the club could have made, and certainly for me it was life changing. Four months after the day I interviewed Ken for the job, we were together in life and in football—and yes, I can still take care of myself. We also won all five trophies on offer in 2008.

A triumphant start to a successful period of football for the club.

Some years later, Ken and I were married. Our six children were delighted with our choice of wedding arrangements. A quick visit to the registry office in Melbourne, a delicious lunch at the Hyatt and then a stroll to AAMI Park to a private box for the Melbourne City vs Melbourne Victory derby. What else does a football family do on their wedding day?

Partnerships are important in football. Look at the strength of a good centre back pairing or two strikers working together. I have a partnership with our senior coach and with South Hobart Football Club. At 112 years old, Tasmania's oldest Association Football club and one of the oldest in Australia is feeling her age and her needs are great. She is a place of comfort for so many, a weekly catch-up with friends, an opportunity to spend time with your children, to scream loudly, cheer or feel that gut-wrenching knot in your stomach after a loss.

Our home ground is South Hobart Oval. As only the southern states of Australia can do, they call our rectangle an oval. Over the past decade the ground has been renamed colloquially D'Arcy Street by most familiar with it. The lower side of the ground borders D'Arcy Street. I think football people like to call it D'Arcy because it doesn't insinuate any links to AFL. Some years ago, the club board decided to rename our club South Hobart Football Club. We were formally known as South Hobart Soccer Club. As we grew stronger, we felt there was no need to explain what type of ball we kicked. Our football was certainly proud and strong enough to get on with being who we were and what we did.

As year followed year and my immersion in the football club grew, the club wrapped its fingers around me; we have become one. If she suffers, so do I, and if she celebrates, so do I. Each victory is uplifting and each defeat or setback painful. I believe the club is a direct reflection of myself and those who work with me to make sure she is a place for all. Kindness is essential because she is a place of refuge for so many. She provides time out from the strains of a busy life, she introduces you to new friends, new lovers and families who provide her next generation of football players.

Interesting how the choices you make in life shape those around you. Joining

South Hobart FC and partnering with a professional football coach rubbed off on my own three sons. Two have Asian Football Confederation (AFC) Advanced A Licence coaching qualification and the third a C Licence. The two lads who have A Licences have teaching degrees because it complements their coaching qualifications. Not the other way around. Would they have been plumbers if I had married a plumber? I'm not sure, but certainly our dinnertime meals always involve football, perhaps a more interesting topic than talking about other potential professions.

My nerves are stretched to breaking point on match days. It follows the household build-up which starts straight after the finish of the last game. Who is fit, who will dominate our next opponent, who did well and who did not so well? These conversations continue throughout the week until the squad is named. I don't go there. Choosing the squad is not my job. Of course I hear conversations and express the odd comment: *"Oh really, he will be disappointed."* I keep myself to myself and I never know who is starting a senior game. It is not the president's job to choose the team. I need to make sure we get club, community and culture right on and off the field, but I must trust our coaches to make the right decision.

I like to keep to myself on match day and just watch the football. Talking means I might miss something. As I became more and more invested in our senior results, I started taking photos on match day. It keeps me busy. It doesn't stop the anguish if we lose, but it helps if I get that perfect shot. I have a decade of photos of my club. Children who came as juniors are now playing National Premier League. I have seen them grow up through the lens of my camera.

Loving our football in a state perceived to be dominated by Australian Rules is downright unfair. Advocating for football and my club in Tasmania has been more difficult and unfair than any other journey I have undertaken. I have added other voluntary roles to my football advocacy. Vice chair of the Association of Australian Football Clubs, president of the largest Junior Association in Hobart, and secretary of Women in Football Australia. Sometimes it feels like I'm banging my head against a brick wall. No one seems to listen or see the volume of children playing soccer in Tasmania. Seriously, one only need drive around Hobart on a

Saturday morning to see every school and council ground groaning with junior Sam Kerrs and budding Socceroos. Are politicians blind?

Recently, sadly I attended the funeral of Brian Roberts. Brian and his brother Keith have been part of South Hobart FC for 50 years. Fifty years at our club! They have kept our records and history alive. Brian died suddenly. I had talked to him about a week before his death. He was my go-to man.

What should I do about this? What do you think, Brian? Can you remember who this guy was from the 1950s? Brian went into hospital for respite care and was fully expected by all to come home. His family reported that the night before he died peacefully in his sleep, he watched our NPL game on the live stream because he knew how important the game was for the club. This is what clubs mean to people. I will miss him greatly.

The Medics

Bill Kirkup

(Newcastle United FC)—Former Associate Chief Medical Officer, UK

Bill Kirkup is a medical doctor who has a distinguished record of public service in health administration and public health. He has undertaken notable work in the sphere of health service inquiries. He has been appointed by the United Kingdom Government to lead investigations into several high-profile failures in health systems.

There is a particular football connection to this latter element of Bill's work in that he was the medical expert on the Hillsborough Independent Panel. This panel was set up by the British Government to investigate the Hillsborough disaster.[9] The panel's report led directly to the new inquests which completely exonerated Liverpool FC supporters of any blame or responsibility.

Following graduation from the University of Oxford, his specialist medical

---

9 The Hillsborough disaster occurred at an FA Cup semi-final between Liverpool and Nottingham Forest in April 1989 at the Hillsborough Stadium in Sheffield, England. Shortly before the game started a lack of police control caused severe overcrowding in one area of the stadium occupied by Liverpool supporters. The resulting crush caused 97 deaths. The worst disaster in the history of British sport and led to fundamental changes in stadium design and safety regulations.

training was in the field of obstetrics and gynaecological oncology. He went on to forge a career in several senior positions in public health. He was Associate Chief Medical Officer in the UK between 2005 and 2009. A notable aspect of Bill's activities is his civilian volunteer work in areas of conflict—being involved in public health and reconstruction in Kosovo in 1999, Baghdad in 2003 and 2005, and Afghanistan in 2007 to 2008.

He was made a Commander of the Order of the British Empire (CBE) in 2008, for services to public health.

In *Football Fans,* Bill recounts the story of his lifelong affinity with Newcastle United. He educates us too, as we learn that the much-talked-about bitter rivalry with neighbours Sunderland is a relatively new phenomenon. His story was written three months before the takeover of the Newcastle club.

Supporting Newcastle United

I was born in Newcastle-upon-Tyne a few years after the end of World War Two, a time when rationing was just about ending and interest in football was rekindling. In the North East, that meant Newcastle United and Sunderland. The 'and' may surprise some, but in those days the friendly local rivalry had yet to turn ugly. Many people followed both clubs and almost all would wish both well. My grandfather, although born in West Auckland in South West Durham, favoured Newcastle United and so did my parents, both raised in South Shields—but without animosity to anyone else.

My earliest football memory was of watching the 1955 FA Cup final on a very small cabinet television that we had acquired for the Coronation two years previously. It was hard to follow the grainy pictures, but I knew that Newcastle had won. Later, probably the next day, my grandfather and father came home from Wembley, very obviously still elated but pretending to grumble because Jackie Milburn had scored Newcastle's first goal before they had got into the stadium. I wanted to understand this strange joy and celebration and experience it for myself.

That dream was to take another ten years to become a reality. My father left home, and my grandfather was bedridden for several years, and died 40 years after surviving the trenches of the Great War. My mother was cautious and forbade me from going to a match with no adult male to supervise. Eventually, a school friend suggested that she might relent if we went together, so in January 1965 I went to my first match.

I know what it is supposed to have been like: all those descriptions of the first glimpse of the emerald-green sward through the swaying mass of humanity, the anticipation and emotion of the moment ... All I can say is that St James's Park on a cold January day had not read the script. The Leazes End, which my school friend preferred, resembled a large, half-derelict shed, with a few hundred mostly young men scattered about. This was about 90 minutes before kick-off—3 p.m. on a Saturday, of course—because it was important to get there early enough to get a good spot. That meant in front of a safety barrier, never behind, where you would be pushed forwards against it. The pitch was hardly green at all, being mostly mud, the remaining patches of grass more gunmetal than emerald.

The ground filled gradually, until around ten minutes before kick-off it was impressively full, not just the end where we were but the Gallowgate opposite, the popular side to the left and the main stand. The records say the gate that day was just over 37,000, but I'm pretty sure we used to undercount in those days. Although the Leazes End was filled to the point that moving about was impossible, there was no sense of danger, just keen anticipation of the approaching kick-off.

Our opponents were Cardiff City, in an English (old-style) Second Division match. From the start, I was completely engrossed in the game, and carried along with the sense of belonging, part of a crowd with a single purpose, to encourage Newcastle to a win. When Dave Hilley, a talented but underrated inside forward, scored just before half time, the joy, and the relief of tension temporarily dissipated, were overwhelming. When Stan Anderson, an equally talented halfback, added the second, there was a sense of completion. It certainly wasn't a Cup final, but at last I had experienced those emotions, that tension and finally the elation. I was hooked.

Newcastle were chasing promotion back to the First Division that season, and a win away against Preston North End ensured we were still top when our next home game kicked off. We were playing Ipswich Town, and I was back in front of a barrier in the Leazes End. A goal from Alan Suddick put us ahead early on, and he would quickly become a hero to many of the younger supporters—a local lad of a similar age, in a modern era he would have been 'one of our own'. Although Ipswich equalised in the second half, Newcastle looked to have got a late winner through Stan Anderson. But two minutes later, delight turned to crushing disappointment as Ipswich equalised again, and the match finished 2–2. That was my first experience of the capacity of football to raise its supporters hopes only to dash them again in a moment. There would be many more over the years.

The next week, we lost away to Leyton Orient, and things became more fraught as we went two goals down at home to Bury. A thrilling fightback saw us score twice in eight minutes through Suddick and Anderson to level the game midway through the second half. But in another of those abrupt reversals, Bury scored a very late winner to ruin our hopes of at least a point. We dropped to second place in the division, and nerves began to jangle. There was some discussion that I might be an albatross bringing poor fortune and had better stay at home. Powerful though superstition is among football supporters, I was determined not to cave in, and continued to attend every home game. Fortunately, results improved again from that low, and an unbeaten run of six games found us in position to clinch promotion on Good Friday.

That game was against Bolton Wanderers, and I was in the usual spot even earlier as it was clear there would be a capacity crowd. The official attendance was exactly 40 short of the maximum permitted gate of 60,000, which I found suspicious even then, and the actual crowd was certainly more. The mood among the crowd was laced with a strong sense of anxiety: a win would give us promotion, but Bolton were strong opponents chasing promotion themselves.

For most of the first half we were run ragged by a wonderful centre-forward, Wyn Davies. He would later become a favourite at St James's Park and terrify

European defences in Newcastle's Fairs Cup winning season four years later, but that day he was playing for the opposition, and he had the beating of our defence. He was tall and powerful, but what really set him apart was his ability to jump higher than seemed possible, *'the footballer who could fly'*, and head the ball hard and accurately. He got to almost every cross Bolton put in, and made several alarmingly close chances. With anxiety levels rising, we began to fear that this was not going to be our day. But somehow, after half an hour, Willie Penman scored for Newcastle. I saw him move towards the ball, but immediately he struck it the pitch was entirely hidden from my view by an eruption of leaping, cheering supporters. With a one-goal lead the tension remained high, but we managed to hang on until half time.

Newcastle's manager was Joe Harvey, veteran of two FA Cup-winning sides of the 1950s, and it is said that he asked at half time for a harder approach to Davies, saying *"Let's see how fast he can limp."* Whether or not these were the instructions, we had no idea in the Leazes End, but we did have a fine view of our centre half, John McGrath, following Wyn Davies out near the touch line and crashing into him with a tackle that left him lying on the cinder track. After treatment, he was just about able to resume—no substitutes then—but it turned out that he didn't limp so fast, nor jump so high. Jim Iley scored a second for Newcastle; it was at the far end, and I saw little of that goal either as thousands in the Leazes End began celebrating the moment he hit the shot. The celebrations went on to the final whistle and, with promotion assured, well beyond.

The rest of the season passed more sedately with three draws, the last a 0–0 at home to Manchester City that gave us the Second Division title. I was not naïve enough to think that all the seasons to come would be as exciting or ultimately as rewarding as that one, but I did hope for a share of success. After all, Liverpool had come back to the First Division only two years previously and were already in the process of founding a dynasty that would last a couple of decades. Newcastle were as well supported, so why not, we thought, but the reality turned out to be all about squandered opportunities, interspersed with the odd bout of unreasonable hope. For better or mostly worse, however, once a supporter always a supporter: of course Newcastle United remains my team 56 years on, and I'm still in what used to be the Leazes End for home games, virus permitting. My guilty secret is that the answer to the question *"When do you feel happiest?"* is *"Walking down Barrack Road after a decent home win to celebrate with friends."* Well, the scarcity value makes it all the sweeter.

Sir Jonathan Van-Tam
(Boston United FC)—
Former Deputy Chief Medical Officer, UK; Epidemiologist

I live in Australia, and I sometimes watch the Sky News UK channel on satellite TV. During the COVID-19 pandemic the announcer would cross to the news conference briefing room in Downing Street (the residence of the UK prime minister in London). After the politicians, Sir Jonathan Van-Tam would step up to the lectern to deliver the daily expert briefing: expert in the sense of the medical update. Explaining the situation to the UK population—urging them to get vaccinated and outlining best practice for prevention. What caught my attention was that he always seemed to be using football analogies to make his point.

Here's a few samples:

"We started off with 11 players but we've picked up a couple of injuries."

"... but with Alpha and Delta we've had to use a couple of subs."

"Omicron—it's like we've picked up a couple of yellow cards. We might beat it, but we might go down to ten men. We're not going to wait for the red card."

Thinking of my endeavours in recruiting contributors for the book I thought, *"I've got to look up this guy. He has to be a football fan. Who does he support, I wonder?"* He underscored it when in one briefing he announced, *"People are relaxing at the wrong time. It's like being 3 nil up and thinking, 'We can't possibly lose now!', but how many times have you seen the other side take it 4–3?"* A little bit of digging and I found that he is a lifelong supporter of Boston United—National League North in England (the sixth tier).

He was charged with presenting those briefings in his capacity as deputy chief medical officer, a role he was appointed to in late 2017. This is a role open only to senior public health professionals and the appointment is made on a competitive basis. In Sir Jonathan's case we might aver that it was a prescient, if not lucky choice. His research specialism is in influenza and other respiratory viruses. He is a world recognised expert in epidemiology and pandemic preparedness. He was already in post and played a leading role in the United Kingdom's response when COVID-19 came along.

Before taking up the deputy CMO role, he was Professor of Health Protection at the University of Nottingham. He led a World Health Organisation Collaborating Centre for pandemic research.

He has received many honours across his career and is an esteemed member of various public health-related learned societies and a Fellow or Honorary Fellow of many royal medical colleges. He is honorary chair of the Vietnamese Intellectual Society in the UK and Ireland. He was knighted in 2022 for services to public health.

He stepped down from the deputy CMO role in March 2022, returning to Nottingham to a position as pro-vice chancellor at the university.

In my research for this introduction, I discovered that he delivered several CV vaccinations to members of the Boston United squad. It was quite charming to read that, whilst he was the celebrity, as it were, like any fan he confessed to being starstruck at such a responsibility.

In his piece for *Football Fans* Sir Jonathan recounts the history of why he follows the Pilgrims. What is it that caused him to be 'rusted on' and keeps him there?

The Pilgrims

When you grow up in the small market town of Boston in Lincolnshire (by the way this is the original Boston as opposed to the large U.S. city named after the former), it doesn't take long before you realise that there are no English Premier League clubs anywhere close. Leicester City is the nearest club with established PL status and at the time of writing Nottingham Forest (last in the top flight in 1993) have just made it back. This leaves the two major clubs in the town: Boston United or Boston Town, the former being much bigger than the latter.

I can't say I made a deliberate choice to be a Boston United fan. Like so many other fanatical fans around the world, and like so many of our career choices in life, there's usually a bit of happenstance involved. For me this came in two parts. The first was my dear grandad: Lionel Thompson, or 'Bomp' as he was known in the family. Bomp was a wharf agent for Anderson's at the dock. He was also a keen football fan—Swansea City (his boyhood side) and, of course, Boston United. He started taking me to matches when I was about seven years old. I can place this precisely, because Jim Smith and Howard Wilkinson were some of the players I knew before they became famous elsewhere. To this list was added John Froggatt in 1969–74 and Jim Kabia in 1974, both of whom couldn't stop scoring. However, Jim Kabia was extra special to me because he also worked on Boston Dock, cementing his connection to my grandad's place of work.

The second part was York Street—home to the iconic and original stadium. This was also where my great-great aunt, Florence Johnson (aka 'Auntie Florrie'), lived, at No. 13. Those familiar with our old stadium will know that No. 13 York Street is on the same side of the road as the stadium and maybe four doors away. In those days, cycling everywhere was very much the norm in Boston and so leaving our bikes in Auntie Florrie's yard became the thing to do. This was the case for Saturday home games at 3 p.m. and evening fixtures.

We used to take along my best friend Graham Cowie to most of the games. We always sat in the main stand, except on the day when Derby County F.C. came to town (more on this later). Looking back on those now distant memories a few things stand out for me. First, the construction of the place never really changed in my supporting lifetime and was the same as my boyhood memories when we finally left for our new home in 2020. Second, the intense rivalry between Boston United and Kettering Town F.C. which persists to this day. Third, the immense joy as a child of watching Jim Kabia, my all-time BUFC hero, banging goal after goal (101 goals in 240 appearances). And finally, the overwhelming experience of the FA Cup third round replay at York Street against Derby County in 1974. A disappointing result but I have never seen the stadium so full, and we kids had to sit on the grass near the touchlines as for sure we would have been crushed in the stands. In the 1970s Boston United were a seriously successful club and we were more often Northern Premier League champions than not. These were my happy childhood memories of a club that helped cement its position as a big part of my life, and now my family's.

From 1980 to 2000 I was studying hard to try to get into medical school, then in medical school, and finally a junior doctor. The hours were horrendous, weekends were very rarely completely off, and getting to Boston United was sporadic and difficult. But in 2000, I found the space in my life to resume attendance at Boston United in a serious way, and I've been a season ticket holder ever since.

This was in the middle of the Steve Evans managerial era. Like the majority of fans at the time, I had no understanding or inkling of any untoward matters away from the pitch but enjoyed the obvious success on it. In my view, Mr Evans had a definite eye for selecting great players and he could really motivate them. I suppose that era culminated in one of the most memorable and enjoyable days of my BUFC life: the trip to Hayes FC in 2002 and promotion to the Football League. For some reason (perhaps by deliberate scheming) I found myself car-less in Boston on that fateful Sunday. I'd booked the supporters' bus for the trip down but, living in Hertfordshire at the time, the bus dropped me off at the Welwyn Garden City roundabout on the A1 on the way home. Nothing mattered that day except that my team from a small market town in Lincolnshire had made it to the Football League and I had been there to see it. We were now truly (as the song goes) *"... a massive club."*

In the years that followed I made the trip every fortnight from Hertfordshire to Boston, usually with my young daughter in tow (she was also a true Pilgrim for much of her childhood). Up the A1 in the morning, park on Rowley Road (outside my sister's house) lunch in the town, head for the game, back down the A1 afterwards and then a curry at Codicote Spice in the evening. Legendary moments when me and my daughter made so many shared memories that will stay with us for a lifetime. We'll never forget those home and away games versus Lincoln City and the small plastic stool that went with us to the games so that she could see over the hoardings.

When the financial troubles became apparent, it was a truly grim and desperate time. Firstly, I started to mourn in advance what seemed to be the inevitable loss of an institution that had meant so much to me as child and had come to mean so much to me again, this time with my own child. How could three generations of shared love of the same football club die? In desperation I took out membership at Notts County, Nottingham Forest and Peterborough United (POSH) as precautionary measures so there would be football to go to the next season. Confessions here:

1) I could not bring myself to join Lincoln City (sorry!).

2) I still go to the POSH once or twice every season as my mum lives out that way now, and London Road is a grand old stadium.

Nowadays Boston United is a truly 'baked in' part of my life. I've been a season ticket holder for over 20 years. My daughter is grown up now but in her place are my two boys who after years of 'training' are also die-hard fans; their mother (my wife) joined us as a regular five or six years ago and so the whole weekend is planned around whether Boston are home or away. We've had some great family away days, or away weekends, thanks to BUFC. Favourites are probably Southport (superb chips and gravy), Bradford Park Avenue (don't miss out on the samosas), Rochdale (the Cemetery Pub) and Gainsborough Trinity (a very high-quality steak pie). Recently me and my eldest son had a great football weekend in Morpeth; drive up Friday night, beers and a hotel, Park Run at Newbiggin, breakfast then drive to Morpeth Town AFC. Shame about the result, but the ups and downs of the FA Trophy are what following Boston is all about.

The desire to watch football has taken me to some exotic locations including Kilmarnock FC (newly promoted to the Scottish Premier League), SV Darmstadt, Galatasaray, Toronto FC, Chicago Fire, Whitby Town F.C, Belenenses SAD, FC Porto, the Champions League Final 2009 for Barcelona v Manchester United in Rome and Turkmenistan vs Indonesia. I'm very much a football match opportunist. However, I am a Boston United fan at heart. Nothing ever changes that, including the unexpected public profile of the last few years. At the Department of Health and Social Care, since late 2017 they have all known I am a Boston United die hard. Someone even nicked my BUFC mug from the old kitchen at Richmond House! They know that my weekends are dominated by 'the game' and know to check the scores on a Monday morning to predict how I will feel. It was a completely natural thing to wear a BUFC tie at Number 10 Downing Street for one of the Coronavirus Press Briefings. The fans went mad, and I believe Boston United were trending in the top ten on Twitter for a short time. Some poor unfortunate souls claimed it was an old school tie or even a club in Hampshire; those claims were quickly shot down.

Football analogies have become my stock in trade for explaining complex science concepts related to COVID-19; I watch so much football, it comes rather naturally. The pandemic years have been hard. I remember a superb victory at home to York City FC on February 8, 2020. The world was going mad by this stage. A friend from the Department of Health and Social Care (DHSC) came up for the weekend to attend the game; I felt it would be the last football for some time. My friend spent all Sunday morning (from about 4 a.m.) in our kitchen supervising one of the UK evacuation flights from Wuhan City. When football finally returned in person, the welcome from my friends at the stadium was quite overwhelming. I thank them all for the warmth and support I received. It was great to finally bookend the worst of the pandemic with yet more DHSC friends invited back to the new stadium in 2020 (including 'the boss': Sir Chris Whitty—the Chief Medical Officer).

Boston United deserve to be playing in the National League. One day soon, we will get there. Two play-off final defeats in quick succession, in 2021 and 2022, will soon enough be followed by promotion. But the best bit about football is that after the memories of the euphoria and the angst of the last season have faded, it all begins again with the build-up to another eagerly anticipated season. And so, the dream goes on ……. Boston 'til I die!

The Politicians

Lord David Blunkett
(Sheffield Wednesday FC)—Former MP, member of the House of Lords

David Blunkett is a former MP in the House of Commons where, as a member of the Labour Party, he represented the constituency of Sheffield Brightside and Hillsborough from 1987 to 2015.

Prior to entering Parliament, he had extensive experience at local government level on the Sheffield City Council.

He had a distinguished career as an MP and commanded respect from both sides of the House. Before the Labour Party came to government in 1997, he held shadow ministerial roles. In the government led by Tony Blair he was appointed as a cabinet minister, first as Secretary of State for Education and Employment followed by spells leading the Home Office and, lastly, Work and Pensions. His achievements as a minister were many. Notable among them was a huge increase in higher education with significantly increased investment in universities. He introduced the Sure Start program providing support services for families with pre-school children. In the late 1990s, under his education portfolio, he introduced the literacy and numeracy program and the teaching of citizenship in schools (referred to as civic education in some jurisdictions).

After standing down from his seat in the House of Commons he was made a life peer taking the title Baron Blunkett of Brightside and Hillsborough in the City of Sheffield.

He holds a professorship in Politics in Practice at the University of Sheffield and is a Fellow of The Academy of Social Sciences. He has two notable publications to his name, both autobiographical. *On a Clear Day* published in 1995 and *The Blunkett Tapes: My Life in the Bear Pit* in 2006.

In *Football Fans,* David Blunkett explains why he is enchanted by Sheffield Wednesday. He has followed the Owls for as long as he can remember—home and away. In my research for this book, I found a story of him meeting up with a friend at Stamford Bridge—a capacity crowd to see Wednesday away at Chelsea. What is special about meeting a friend amongst the milling throng outside a football ground? David Blunkett has been blind since birth—just like the friend he was looking for.

What Football Means to Me

When, at the age of four, I visited the Hillsborough football ground for the first time, I never thought for a moment about not being able to see the game.

My dad sat me on the wall behind the goal. In those days, of course, you could do that! The tragedy that was to occur at the other end of the ground, 38 years later was, quite simply, unimaginable. There were no pens, and no wire fencing, preventing people from pouring onto the pitch. The 70,000 fans (because that was the capacity of the ground at the time) came for camaraderie, for the spectacle and to escape the drudgery of 12-hour shifts at work.

Remember, in those days, clubs would play on Christmas Day at home, and on the following day, Boxing Day, they would be playing away against the same team. Injuries were run off, players got up when they were tripped, and because of the weight of the ball, much of the game was played on the ground rather than on the head.

I digress. Those heady days as a youngster going to Hillsborough got me hooked. I was to be an Owls supporter for the rest of my life. The sound of the crowd gave the immediate understanding, from the noise, as to whether we were on the attack, likely to score or to be scored against, and brought all this alive.

All these years later, sitting in the South Stand, I now have a commentary, over earphones, provided by local volunteers. All of this supplemented by either my wife Margaret, or one of my sons—as I tend to always be accompanied to the game. And when, as so often happens now on Radio 5, the commentary drifts off into comment (expert observations), there is always someone there to keep me updated as to what's happening on the pitch.

My now long-dead half-brother, Derek, was a groundsman at Hillsborough when I was growing up. The pitch has always been a challenge as it slopes down towards the Kop End with a particular corner that has a dip which the home side should be familiar with, to give them an advantage over the away team. Sadly, not too often!

In fact, the dip was so great that when, in 2007, Sheffield was hit badly by the floods, that part of the pitch was under several feet of water, and when the pitch was replaced, some effort was made to reduce the differential.

I'm often asked, as someone who can't see, precisely what it is that I get out of the game. Of course, it makes an enormous difference to have a team to support. Whilst I'm interested in football in general, and listen to commentaries on Radio 5 and TalkSport, it is my team, Sheffield Wednesday, that make or break a Saturday afternoon.

Following football is not an interest, it's a passion. In fact, it becomes an obsession. I'm afraid, like politics, it gets into the blood, and no matter how often I proclaim that I can't put up with the disappointments any longer, I do!

Just like politics, and for that matter, love, football has its major ups and downs. One minute it lifts you, as your team pull out all the stops and manage that win you never expected. They take you to Wembley (the last time Wednesday were there was in 2016 for the Championship play-off), and then they take you to the depths. On that fateful day when we could have reached the Premier League, we lost 1–0 to Hull City. A tea-time kick-off with the team having been confined in the Wembley Hotel, just across the road, for the previous 24 hours. As a know-all, an amateur psychiatrist and, of course, shadow football manager, I thought it was a mistake from the beginning. The players needed to be out in the fresh air, kicking a ball about and having a bit of banter. The last thing they needed was to be confined to a hotel. But what do I know?

Prior to that we'd been to Wembley in '91 and '93, and the famous (well, famous to Sheffield Wednesday supporters) 1966 Cup final. Yes, there was another major event in 1966, as well as the World Cup!

I was listening to it on the radio because I was still at a school for the blind in Shropshire. When we were 2–0 up, I was literally on my feet. But I should have known better. Raymond Glendenning, the great and enthusiastic commentator, brought the bad news that turned a great day into sadness. Everton won 3–2.

I wrote to the then manager, and the team agreed to come over to the school near Shrewsbury. A great day for me, because so many of the players were well known, and they gave their time freely. In fact, I remember a Scottish player by the name of McCalliog heading a ball further than I could kick it.

So here we are, in League One for the second season, having failed in the 2021/22 play-offs against Sunderland. This season, welcoming the newly promoted Exeter City, Port Vale, Forest Green Rovers and Bristol Rovers. New grounds to visit, more Saturday evenings to rejoice or, regrettably, to grumble over the evening meal and a compensatory glass of something nice.

For as Bill Shankly, former great Liverpool manager, quite rightly put it—this is not just a game, it's life or death!

Sir Lindsay Hoyle
(Bolton Wanderers FC)—Speaker of the House of Commons, UK

Sir Lindsay Hoyle is the Speaker of the House of Commons in the United Kingdom Parliament. He succeeded John Bercow as Speaker in 2019. He entered Parliament as the MP for Chorley (in Lancashire) in the 1997 general election – his first as a candidate. Representing the Labour Party, he became Chorley's first Labour MP in 18 years having turned a deficit of some 4,000 at the previous election into a majority of almost 10,000.

There is a tradition in the House of Commons that the Speaker has no party affiliation – on assuming the chair, the incumbent renounces their party membership. Sir Lindsay stated that as Speaker he would be transparent, and the House would change for the better. I recall a demonstration of his resolve in television coverage of a memorable exchange with Boris Johnson. Sir Lindsay's comment went something like: *"You might be the Prime Minister but, in this House, I'm in charge."* Clear enough – transparent indeed!

He lives in his constituency in the town of Adlington where he was born.

Before entering Parliament, he was a local councillor. He took a turn as mayor of Chorley Borough Council in the year before he became an MP.

He was knighted in 2018 for parliamentary and political services.

In *Football Fans,* Sir Lindsay tells us the story of why he follows Bolton Wanderers which sits just outside his parliamentary constituency. The Trotters won the FA Cup the year after Sir Lindsay was born – two semi-finals since.

The Trotters

When asked to contribute to this book my mind turned to my life-long support of Bolton Wanderers.

Many readers will know that Bolton has a long and proud history as a founder member of the Football League in 1888. Of the 12 founder members, six were in the historic county of Lancashire, reminding us of the working-class roots of the sport which were developed from industrial heartlands such as Bolton.

The town's industrial might was matched on the football field as the club became a powerhouse of footballing talent. The team won the FA Cup three times in the 1920s and have appeared in several notable finals. Most famously of all they won the 1923 "White Horse" final against West Ham, remembered more for scenes prior to kick off. This was the first final ever held at the newly built Wembley Stadium (then styled as the Empire Stadium). Vast crowds surged into the stadium, far exceeding Wembley's 125,000 capacity. Mounted police tried to disperse the crowds. The image of the police officer on a white horse in front of thousands of fans became the enduring image of the day.

Bolton remained in the top flight uninterrupted between 1935-1964 and boasted one of England's finest ever strikers – Nat Lofthouse. Nat is a legend of the game, scoring 30 goals in 33 games for England, helping Bolton to be a major force in football and leading the club to victory in the 1958 FA Cup Final over arch rivals Manchester United.

He also played in the 1953 Cup Final commonly referred to as the 'Matthews Final'. Nat helped Bolton take a 3-1 lead in the game. His goal after a mere 75 seconds meant that he scored in every round of that year's FA Cup. Unfortunately for Bolton, their left half, Eric Bell, was injured early in the game and left hobbling on the wing. These were the days before substitutions and Bolton were left to play the rest of the game with 10 fit men. As the game progressed and tiredness kicked in, the extra space on the pitch allowed Matthews and his teammates (in particular Stan Mortensen who scored a hat trick – another often overlooked fact from that game) to find their stride and win the game 4-3. Had the injury not occurred the outcome may have been different, but such are the twists of fate on which history and legends are made.

Bolton's footballing pedigree is second to none. Against this backdrop I followed my father and started to support Bolton as a youngster. Whilst the club has not reached the heights of the success outlined above, we have experienced highs and lows and provided many memorable moments. could refer to Bolton's time in the Premier League between 2001-2012 and the magnificent 2005 season when they finished 6th and qualified for the UEFA Cup for the first time in their history.

However, having reflected on my time as a Wanderers fan one moment stands out in my mind as the greatest and most memorable. For some people, it may be a particular season, for others a wonderful game, but I would like to focus on one goal!

The goal came on 21st April 1979. Bolton played host to Ipswich Town in the old First Division at their former ground, Burnden Park. The moment of breathtaking skill was courtesy of Bolton's maverick striker Frank Worthington.

One of the game's greatest entertainers, Frank became a cult hero at Burnden Park during the late 1970s.

Frank's professional career began at Huddersfield Town before signing for Leicester City. During this time he won 8 England caps and scored 72 goals in 210 league appearances for the Foxes.

His move to Burnden Park came in September 1977 where he scored on his debut against Stoke City. He helped the club win the Second Division Championship in 1978, scoring the winning goal at Blackburn Rovers that secured promotion, and the following season he was the leading scorer in the First Division.

But his skill on the pitch was only to be surpassed by his flair off the pitch. Frank was a huge Elvis fan and was known to dress up as the King, even when turning up for training. He was a great entertainer, stylish and popular with players and fans alike.

Frank's flair on the pitch was highlighted in the most spectacular fashion at Burnden Park on that April afternoon. Thankfully the game was televised so millions could enjoy the moment of magic, and this can still be viewed today.

The goal came in the first half as Bolton's Alan Gowling headed the ball to Frank who, stood on the edge of the penalty area with his back to the goal, received the ball with a nudge of his head as it bounced up, juggled it twice, flicked it over his shoulder, turned around and volleyed the ball into the back of the net. Sensational!

The Burnden faithful were euphoric, the opposition stunned, and having witnessed the goal live you instantly knew you had watched something very special. Perhaps a true reflection of how breathtaking the goal was can be measured by the fact that the referee can be seen applauding as he makes his way back to the halfway line!

Even now, having seen the goal replayed many times, it leaves one in awe at the exceptional skill involved. It was worthy of Pelé, Maradona or Messi. There are great goals which come from fantastic team efforts, where great players combine to produce something special. Then there are goals which come from absolutely nothing and are pure genius on behalf of one individual. Frank's goal was definitely the latter.

Having seen the goal and read about it some may ask the question, but who won the game? The answer was Ipswich who secured an important 2-3 victory. Not only did Ipswich win but two of the three goals came from the boot of Alan Brazil – and both were fine goals. Indeed, on any other day they would have been the centre of attention. Indeed, Brazil was quoted as saying: "I scored two of the best goals of my career that day, but no one remembers them because of Frank's."

I think it speaks volumes about the quality of Frank's goal that it completely overshadowed the result and Alan's best efforts.

Not surprisingly Frank's heroics were rewarded as this moment of magic was recognised as the goal of the season in a vote conducted by the UK's ITV channel. During that season Frank beat Liverpool's Kenny Dalglish as the First Division's top goal scorer – a testament to his outstanding form at that time.

Frank Worthington played his final game for the club in a scoreless home draw with Arsenal and in October 1979 joined Birmingham City for £150,000. He was top scorer at St Andrew's and had summer loan spells with Mjällby and Tampa Bay Rowdies before joining Leeds United in 1982 for £100,000.

He later spent time with Sunderland, Brighton, Tranmere – where he became player-manager – Preston North End and Stockport County. Of his 38 goals for Bolton the strike against Ipswich was undoubtedly the best and most memorable and probably the best goal scored at Burnden Park.

Frank sadly passed away in 2021 and tributes poured in from far and wide from past players, friends, fans, and current day footballing heroes. He was a pure entertainer, a maverick on and off the field. His place in Bolton Wanderers folklore is truly cemented and his unique talent remembered by many.

Thank you, Frank, for providing me and many Bolton fans with so many happy memories, so many stories to tell and one truly unique and outstanding moment of footballing magic!

Joan Walley

(Port Vale FC)—Former Member of the House of Commons, UK

Between 1987 and 2015 Joan Walley was the Member of Parliament, representing the Labour Party, for Stoke-on-Trent North in Staffordshire. It is the constituency where Port Vale Football Club is located and, like Joan, where I was born and grew up. Joan was educated at the University of Hull and the University College of Wales. Prior to entering the House of Commons, Joan had a career in local government administration and charitable organisations.

In addition to her day-to-day work as an MP, Joan was involved in various House of Commons committees and chaired the Environmental Audit Committee for five years.

After retiring from her parliamentary position, she was appointed to the UK's Electoral Commission—a body that regulates election procedures and political party finances. She is a Deputy Lieutenant (DL) of Staffordshire, a position supporting the King's representative (the Lord Lieutenant) in ceremonial matters in the county.

Her piece in *Football Fans* tells a story that may be familiar to many local politicians. Often, they are rank-and-file football fans too. However, because of the potential influence they possess it often falls to them to support their club in the corridors of power. It highlights the trials and tribulations of the lower leagues. Of shoestring budgets, the hand-to-mouth existence which belies the fact that they operate in the same market as the 'big name' clubs. A situation that was only accentuated by the broadcasting rights deals struck in the advent of the English Premier League.

It is a story that is not uncommon to many clubs in the lower leagues. It takes on extra spice with references to intra-community rivalries in two team cities, and where one received better local government support than the other.

Saving the Valiants

It was back in 1985.

We were nearing the end of the interviews to select the Labour Party candidate to stand for the Stoke-on-Trent North constituency in the forthcoming general election (for the UK Westminster Parliament).

Long gone, but I can still see him now in his prime, as real as you and me. A big, warm bear of a man, always there when needed and when it counted with his big, broad shoulders and rich baritone voice. A socialist, a much loved and respected trade union leader. Almost as an afterthought he asked, *"If we chose you, would you be there for the Vale?"*

Fast forward thirty-five years or so and, as if looking to another match, the way footballers do, to another snapshot of what the Vale means to people here in North Staffordshire. This time I'm with another dear friend but this time for him we are in 'added time', so to speak, as he confronts brutal, terminal cancer. But all our focus is on the giant-sized plastic-coated new season's fixture list propped up at the bottom of the clinical bed in his stark downstairs room. Forget his pain—all we talk about is the new Port Vale squad and the fast-approaching new League Two season. We anticipate and hope that this will be **the** season.

Nothing can actually convey just how much Port Vale FC means to its followers: to the past and present generations of families, singles, youngsters, mates and local business people who take their seat on the terraces or in hospitality boxes as they get behind the team; to its wider community—those in the red-bricked terraced streets straddling the Hamil[10]; those emptying the pubs in Burslem town centre to snake their way under the gaze of the golden angel on top of Burslem town hall (as some would have it, immortalised by singer and Port Vale fan Robbie Williams), in a last-minute effort to make it in time for kick-off. When Saturday comes to Burslem ST6, Port Vale is the reason for and the place to be.

Its worth transcends balance sheets, creditors, all the bricks and mortar of Vale Park stadium, the home of Port Vale FC, fondly still referred to as the 'Wembley of the North', reflecting the aspirations of the club's custodians who oversaw the move from Hanley to Burslem in 1950. Even the sum total of the accumulated club memorabilia of programs, signed shirts, photos and all manner of art work couldn't put a price on the value of what Port Vale means to its valiant and long-suffering followers. PVFC cuts through its fans and this place like the writing through a stick of Blackpool rock.[11] Home or away, the moment the referee blows the whistle a new lifetime starts; a 90-minute compression of the past accumulated ups and downs of previous league campaigns and Cup competitions, of the hopes for future success and for survival, melted into one. All any fan dares ask is to be there, right there, right then, together and in hope, dreaming of nothing more than you and your team doing your best.

Much as I would love to recollect those ups and downs of all the football

---

[10] Hamil Road forms the southeastern perimeter of the Vale Park precinct. The first house my wife and I owned was among those terraced streets, about 100 metres from the stadium. The closest I've lived other than when I was born at the nearby hospital but a stone's throw away.

[11] Long stick of candy (lolly to Australians) with an embedded pattern running through it—typically the name of a seaside resort; Blackpool in Lancashire being a prime example.

seasons that I have supported the Vale, there are numerous books and accounts of our club's history which detail the remarkable and the unremarkable far better than I ever could. But what those volumes can't do is convey the sheer desperation combined with absolute determination (the high-octane mix) that gripped all those who loved the Vale at that point in the run-up to the millennium when they and their club faced oblivion. Port Vale FC just had to be saved. No two ways about it. It just so happened that when the crisis did erupt it happened on my watch as MP. It felt as though saving the Vale fell on to my shoulders.

Fast track back to that millennium turn—to 1999. Successful, self-made and with an iron grip over his beloved club's finances, local car salesman and lovable rogue in equal parts to many, club owner Billy Bell had steered the club through a good few years of promotions and enough memories to last a lifetime. With a distinctive car for just about every occasion, Billy took great pleasure in polishing up his Rolls Royce for a day out to a lower league match at Huddersfield, or wherever else we happened to be playing away from home. Likewise, he would reserve a cherished Bentley for motoring down to London to see Port Vale at the national stadium at Wembley on the rare occasions when we got to appear in a play-off or Cup final. Memories of the Anglo Italian Cup final against Genoa (1996) bring back images, not just of Billy arriving in style but of the whole team kitted out (just like the big-timers) in immaculate identical suits all personally purchased by the club chairman from the finest bespoke tailors in town. Those were the days when we could summon 20 packed supporters' coaches to take fans to an away fourth-round FA Cup draw at Everton in Liverpool or Elland Road in Leeds (Premier Leaguers both).

Our success on the pitch though was not so much due to the chairman but to the manager. Legendary John Rudge arrived at the club in 1979. His playing career might not have reached the dizzying heights scaled by today's celebrity footballers but backed by his wife Del, this sincere hardworking manager rolled up his sleeves to attend to just about every job going at the club to help get us to winning ways. If the changing room needed painting, the gaffer got out the paintbrush. He was equally proficient at driving hard bargains in his search for skilful footballers to sign for the club. Shrewd and down to earth, he walked a tightrope between lack of money for investment and fielding a team that could take on the best. I well remember arriving at the ground at an away match at Swindon just as John was getting off the team coach. *"Who've we got playing then?"* we asked. Back came the reply that he wasn't sure we could even manage to field a team, injuries and illness being so high. No wonder fundraising is underway in 2022 to create a statue to capture all that he means to the Vale.

Despite Vale's best efforts, lower attendances and correspondingly lower gate receipts were beginning to affect all lower league clubs in the EFL and not just ours. Looking back over decades, a failure in football governance is to blame. Match revenues no longer shared fairly between home and away fixtures; Alan Sugar's casting vote to approve the setting up of the Premier League in English football—such decisions were having a cumulative effect on the financial viability of the football pyramid. At the very least the introduction of the income from broadcasting rights for the new elite Premier League meant a drawbridge had been erected between the top elites and lower leagues. Money simply did not trickle down despite assurances that it would. Clubs grounded in their local communities like Port Vale could no longer compete on a level playing field when it came to football finances.

Meanwhile, changing local circumstances were taking their toll too. Having achieved longed-for success and promotion, ground safety standard requirements meant that higher safety standards applied and our days of standing on the terraces of the Lorne Street Stand were numbered. I spearheaded efforts to secure derogation from all seating arrangements for a couple of seasons, but inevitably the ultimatum came. Convert to all seating or lose the club's safety certificate. Accordingly work to upgrade the Lorne Street stand had to commence. Beset by underground mineshafts and financial difficulties there was no financial help from the government for land remediation. Our efforts to secure European funding to incorporate business units into the stand were more successful, as was a bid to locate and build an onsite children's centre, but this support was not sufficient to enable the Lorne Street stand to be completed. When it reopened in

1999 it was only half complete, leaving half of the lower tier main stand without any seating at all and bereft of spectators. Such necessary investment in stadium safety came to mean even less money for the running of the club and players' wages. Which in turn meant the football and results on the pitch would suffer.

Another significant factor in the club's falling income was the decision of Stoke-on-Trent City Council to close the market (and valuable income stream) that the club was by now operating on its huge car park. Both at the time and in retrospect it was difficult to see why the council would want to harm the club in this way. Yes, there were regulatory matters to address, but nothing that could not have been resolved with common sense on all sides. Yet no amount of pleading could sway the city council. Some local residents complained about the public nuisance from shoppers attending the market and others about lack of adequate toilet facilities. Traders in the town centre complained that a market just walking distance away from Burslem town centre was taking custom out of the town. They cited a centuries-old royal decree which prevented any market other than in the centre of town. Unlikely forces joined together to force through the closure of what had become a gold mine for Port Vale, leaving the club bereft of additional funds brought in by the market to supplement match day income.

Such failure to engage in meaningful dialogue between municipality and club was all the sourer in the light of developments at the other end of the city. Stoke-on-Trent, capital of ceramics and widely known by the nickname the Potteries, is a linear city made up of six pottery towns all spread out like a string of pearls. Founder member of the Football League, the other EFL club in our city, Stoke City FC, has its roots in the town of Stoke after which the municipality takes its name. Friendly rivalry has always characterised relationships between the two clubs, with many families historically alternating between home matches. Other than for short interludes, Stoke City has tended to play in leagues higher than Port Vale leaving the Burslem-based club perceived as the underdog.

Stoke-on-Trent's fortunes had very much turned a corner with the closure of the remaining coal mines in Staffordshire and the Trentham pit in particular. The fight to keep that pit open had been a particularly bitter one. This was in a time which predated the urgent climate emergency negotiations we now know are needed to phase out coal and fossil fuels. The Thatcher government of the day was intent on closing the pits as part of its campaign waged against the miners. At the height of that campaign to stop the pit closure I travelled down to London with the city council leader to make a last-minute plea to Secretary of State Michael Heseltine to save Trentham colliery. As the train picked up speed and pulled out of the station, he turned, pointed to the distant colliery buildings on our left and said, *"Not long now before all that'll be gone and before you know it Stoke City will be playing there."*

I was flabbergasted. To be embarking on a mission to save the pit and at the same time contemplate Plan B even before any decision had been made did not augur well for what we were aiming to achieve—saving jobs, livelihoods and proud mining communities of the North Staffordshire coalfield. Whether his words were wishful thinking or a premonition of what would follow if we failed in our mission to save the pit, I have no idea. His throwaway comments at a time of great strife and tension served only to underline the superior place that his football club commanded in the hearts and minds of the city council. [Maybe it was Plan A all along?! *Ed*].

His words were prescient indeed. In no time at all the mine was shut down, and Stoke-on-Trent City Council and Stoke City FC had engineered a joint venture to build a £14.8 million new, state-of-the-art football stadium well away from their traditional home at the Victoria Ground. Tasked with the regeneration of the former colliery brownfield site, the council had meanwhile secured funding for land remediation and new road infrastructure to service the new football stadium and the other investments which would surely follow. Meanwhile, the arrival of Icelandic investors had secured Stoke City FC's club finances.

On the pitch a rare victory by Port Vale at a local derby match might have boosted their standing but Port Vale's fortunes off the pitch were starting to slide. Worse still, long-serving heroic manager John Rudge had not only exited the club but re-emerged as director of football at Stoke City. There was a sense that whatever Midas touch Port Vale chairman Billy Bell might once have had was starting to fade. Fans were afraid that the unthinkable might happen and were accordingly preparing for their worst nightmare by getting ready and organised in case they needed to rush to its rescue.

Looking back, and from the outside, it is impossible to pinpoint what exactly created the tipping point in what was by now a downward spiral reflected both on and off the pitch at Port Vale. The trigger for me was a phone call one weekend from the chairman telling me that he had put the club into administration almost immediately followed by calls from the press asking for my comments. However inevitable, this news still came as a bombshell and didn't bear thinking about. Players, backroom staff and fans all feared the worst. The chairman meanwhile seemed at this stage to be in denial, so sure was he that by putting the club into administration he had hit upon a holding device that would enable him and the club at the end of the process to make a full return to business as usual. If only it were that simple.

For my part I quickly realised that I needed to be immediately up to speed on all the ins and outs of what it meant for a football club to be in administration, and equally important what it would take to get Port Vale out of administration. Accordingly, I was on the doorstep of the newly appointed administrator's office at 9 a.m. sharp on the Monday morning before travelling down to Westminster.

The detailed conversations that followed filled me with dread. I learnt that administration has a due process all its own and equally important too were the rules relating to football clubs' continued membership of the EFL. The two processes might be quite separate but reaching the finishing line goal of coming out of administration was dependant on satisfactorily completing both due processes. Any slip-up and we risked losing the club altogether. To stay as a going concern and avoid being kicked out of the league, the club had to maintain its continuous league status, which in turn meant fulfilling all its fixture commitments, paying the wages of players and backroom staff, all the while running on empty. It also had to pay the not insignificant fees of the administrator who by now was responsible for all aspects of the running of the club. Not least amongst its woes was the impact the whole saga was having on genuine local businesses who had supplied services in good faith to the club and not been paid. And at the end of this process, a new owner had to be found who could prove sufficient funds to meet the future costs of running a viable club.

The months that followed were a nightmare of uncertainty. The whole future of the club was in the balance. Faced with the crisis, the new manager and players commendably opted to stay at the club regardless of the uncertainty about getting paid and what this might mean for their football careers.

But it was the magnificent, committed supporters who rose to the challenge. Their concern about the way the club was going had long preceded the act of putting the club into administration. Anticipating a crisis, they had formed various fundraising groups to raise money for a crisis they had hoped could be averted. Taking their cue from the Burslem motto, 'Ready', they had hoped for a seamless transition to new ownership. But the administration threatened to put paid to such hopes.

Supporters had even begun to imagine that a supporter-owned club could be the answer and were in touch with people who had led similar successful ventures elsewhere, including at Bournemouth FC. Valiant 2001 emerged as a fan-led group to buy the club out of administration. There were 1000 steps needed if ever the supporters' consortium Valiant 2001 were ever to be in pole position to buy out the club. Looking back on the events of those weeks and months it is incredible to recall the belief, effort and unstinting commitment, not to mention lifetime savings, that so many supporters put into saving the Vale. There were meetings to make and approve the detailed legal arrangements to put Valiant 2001 on to a credible footing as a potential bidder for the club, meetings and fundraising activities based in a former gas company office on High Lane, and a lot of behind-the-scenes work to secure a small amount of funding from Stoke-on-Trent City Council to help produce a business case which could establish the supporters' bid as a viable option when considered alongside other would-be buyers. There was the not insignificant matter of ensuring that the Port Vale Club and the stadium remained as one and could not be sold off separately. And all the time there were matches to be played and games to be won, players to be supported and fans to be mobilised, and all against the mightiest odds.

Every aspect of the fight to save Port Vale was pursued in good faith by those who could not contemplate losing their club. The more the fans considered the likely outcome of administration, the more convinced everyone was that the only future lay in a fan-based ownership model. One that would put the club's interests before any would be outside owner who could not necessarily be trusted to act in the best interests of our football club.

By now I had a clear understanding of the due legal process and as an officer of the All Party Football Group I also knew the requirements of the Football League. Meanwhile rival bidders were circling and finalising their business plans for the purchase of the club. What happened next - had they only known it – would have instilled fear into the hearts of every Port Vale fan. Bolstered by their rising ascendancy, the Icelandic investors in Stoke City had come up with a cunning but secretive plan. Apparently acting on the mistaken assumption that Stoke-on-Trent was too small a population to sustain two football clubs, what better long-term solution than for the Icelandic investors at Stoke City to buy Port Vale, maybe finish the season at Vale Park, and then revert to a ground-sharing arrangement at the out-of-town state-of-the-art new Britannia stadium that was now home to Stoke City FC? Never mind the fact that the Vale was essentially a community club, steeped in local tradition and very much at the heart of Burslem, the mother town of the Potteries. There was seemingly no limit to alternative new profitable uses that Vale Park's treasured 'Wembley of the North' stadium could be put to by any new owners seeking to profit from a future sale of the club and stadium for non-football purposes.

Faced with this proposition, it was difficult to see how it might be resolved. In another era, when the great and the good in the city were contemplating future uses on what became known as 'The Garden Festival' central site of the former shut-down and abandoned steel works at Shelton Bar, a purpose-built and carefully designed city of Stoke-on-Trent football stadium equally accessible to both the north and the south of the city and hence both its league football clubs could have been a possibility. With careful planning and involving the entire football family from grassroots to top flight such a concept maybe could have been 'sold' to both clubs and supporters as an asset for the city around which football could unite. But when the opportunity had arisen such an investment hadn't even been considered. The present proposal from Stoke City's Icelandic owners to invest in and take advantage of a club on its knees was a million miles away from any prospect of a joint Potteries stadium serving both clubs equally.

Over 20 years later and the memories of combined efforts to both save the Vale and avert the sale of the club to the Icelandic investors at Stoke City are still raw. It is humbling to relive the fervent commitment which Vale fans applied to saving their club to avoid the tragedy that has subsequently befallen equally worthy lower league clubs like Bury FC and Macclesfield Town in recent years. Suffice to say that, at the time when all this was being played out, just like in any game of football waiting for the referee's whistle, there was no guaranteeing that Port Vale FC would survive the process of administration intact. This was happening on my watch, and I had to stop the Vale being taken over and to all intents and purposes merged with Stoke City FC. Fortunately, the many years I had served as vice chair of the All Party Parliamentary Football Committee had served me well, building numerous close working relationships with the grandees of English football, including the late Dr Brian Mawhinney, former Tory MP, and by now chairman of the Football League. Despite us being at polar ends of the political divide and crossing swords from across the Dispatch Box of the green benches of House of Commons on all manner of transport policies from port privatisation to new road building, in his new incumbency at the Football League he treated my concerns with the greatest of respect.

The trust I had built with supporters, the administration team at the club and the Football League meant that behind the scenes I was able to arrange for the administrator to brief the chairman of the Football League so as to ensure that account was taken of threats to the long-term survival of Port Vale, paving the way for an outcome of the administration process which had due regard to all factors, not just those of any highest bidder.

In due course the club was sold to supporters' group Valiant 2001. The nightmare was over. At least so it seemed. But then anyone familiar with the words of 'The Port Vale War Cry', dating from the 1920s and released back then to raise money for club funds, would be forgiven for thinking that the trials and tribulations were only just beginning. As indeed they were. But what mattered was the triumph—albeit short-lived—that the club had survived to dream again and to play another season. And for me, all that I could have asked was to have been in the right place at the right time to have the trust that would help create a solution that would save Port Vale.

Little were we to know then that there were to be a few more bitter disappointments and heartbreaking twists and turns along the way and that the longed-for solution for supporters to own their club would go so devastatingly pear-shaped. The 'Port Vale War Cry' song spells it out: "It hasn't been all easy" but no one back then could have imagined we would go on to be embroiled in a saga of nil paid shares by American investors or a controversial second administration that the city council had to be persuaded to fund, or the further breakdown of relations between fans and the club's subsequent owner.

No one should have to experience the threats our club has faced. The governance of English football is quite simply no longer fit for purpose. As we have recently seen with the loss of the aforementioned Bury and Macclesfield Town Football clubs, proper regulation and full enforcement of football in England is long overdue.

Fans at Port Vale have had no choice but to stand up for the club they love by saving it as well as supporting it. It has been a labour of love that at times seemed doomed to failure. Mercifully their fortitude kept the club alive and has been matched by an equally tenacious approach from Carol and Kevin Shanahan which ultimately resulted in their buying the club against all the odds from the subsequent owner.

Port Vale fans at last have their just reward and can hopefully concentrate on the football pitch and their beloved Vale as a true community hub. Their saving grace is that in Carol and Kevin there are now joint owners in place who see their role as custodians of the club for future generations. They have the backing of supporters. Equally important, the English Football League has in Carol an ambassador who can be relied upon not only to do the right thing as far as Port Vale is concerned, but who will be prepared to take on the vested interests inside the world of football. Port Vale's experience can lead the way in safeguarding lower league clubs all over the country whose only ask is to exist on a level playing field.

That presupposes that there is widespread support and not just lip service for UK government backing for radical reform of English football under a new fit-for-purpose regulator. So, let's hope that the fight to save Port Vale will carry on influencing the wider fight for proper (also fit for purpose) governance of football including a fairer share of football's riches for all clubs. Long may the Vale anthem 'The Wonder of You' ring out in ST6 and long may we remember the words of the Port Vale War Cry as a warning and rallying call for football everywhere.

And just in case you thought my tale is all over I want to look forward and back. Back to an entry in a much-treasured autograph book from the 1950s to a page signed by Billy Wright (English footballer, first footballer in the world to earn 100 international caps). *"Always play to the referee's whistle,"* he commands. How he came to sign my dog-eared book is lost in time, but his advice is as timely as ever. In football that hope that this will be the season, this will be our time, that there is still time to get things right, lives on. As it does now. As the 2022 EFL League 2 season draws to a nail-biting close, past, present and future rolls into one. Football transcends the generations. So much so that my seven-year-old granddaughter watching me watching our beloved Port Vale in another end-of-season six-pointer played out on iFollow (the online streaming service) asks,

"Grandma, why is your face so serious when you watch the Vale?"

"Well, because it matters," say I. "You needn't worry," says she. "It's like a fairy tale. It'll have a happy ending."

Acknowledgements

Top of the list, of course, I cannot find adequate words to thank my contributors. Their willingness to reveal their passion for the team they follow has been a joy to behold.

There are many people to thank for their encouragement and support. In this Eddie and Jean Jackson have been a constant, right from the beginning. In the introduction I described how the idea evolved and having Eddie and Jean contribute their memories is illustrative of this. In addition, they did sterling work in helping me with the technical side of reviewing the manuscript and they interviewed Carol Shanahan for her piece. I cannot thank them enough.

In the very early stages of 'shall I, shan't I?' Lisa Clifford and Ailsa Piper, my dear friends and writing mentors, were so enthusiastic about the book. Thank you, thank you.

Thanks to Chris Nikou, Chairman of Football Australia. A contributor himself, and helpful and encouraging all along.

I do want to thank some people who have really helped me to make the book what it is—let me call them the imaginative gatekeepers! Those not mentioned specifically within the text are, in alphabetical order, Kaynat Begum, Davide Chinellato, Nicky Fenton, Joanna Firth, Eileen Hainink, Sophie Jermyn, Emma Lawson, Mimi Robinson, Fiona Petheram, Karen Tighe, Jeremy Stuparich and Peter Wilson.

Bonita Mersiades—what can I say? Thank you, Bonita, in general, for all you do to advance football and to promote the cause of 'really good football books'. Thank you for welcoming me to become part of Fair Play Publishing.

My wife Nicola allows me to 'play around' with this stuff. My love and deep gratitude always.

Photo Credits

Thank you to the individual contributors who supplied photographs from their personal collection.

The photographs sourced elsewhere are:

Page 22:

Ken Loach, Courtesy of Paul Crowther

Page 36:

Pope Francis © Vatican Media

Page 64:

Keith Hackett, PA Images/Alamy Stock Photo

Keith Hackett looks on as Liverpool's Phil Neal and Everton's Kevin Ratcliffe shake hands before the 1984 FA Charity Shield at Wembley.

Page 151:

Sir Jonathan Van-Tam, Courtesy of Downing Street Press Office

Page 159:

Lord David Blunkett © House of Lords. Photograph by Roger Harris

Page 163:

Sir Lindsay Hoyle © House of Commons. Photograph by Jessica Taylor

Page 168:

Joan Walley, Courtesy of *The Sentinel* newspaper, Stoke-on-Trent

About David Picken

David Picken was born in England and is a lifelong supporter of Port Vale now in the English Football League One (third tier) after a stunning play-off victory at Wembley in 2022.

He played competitively from age 11 to 45 in England, Papua New Guinea, Saudi Arabia and Hong Kong. He has been a volunteer women's and junior football coach and an administrator with Surf Coast FC in Victoria, Australia.

In his other life as a construction professional and academic (formerly in Hong Kong and then in Australia at Deakin University) he has published textbooks and scientific papers and won awards for excellence in teaching.

Writing books about football is sheer indulgence. His first, *The Time of My Football Life*, was published by Fair Play Publishing in 2019.

WWW.FAIRPLAYPUBLISHING.COM.AU

PUBLISHED IN SYDNEY

Milton Keynes UK
Ingram Content Group UK Ltd.
UKHW020808171123
432750UK00009B/515